I0822214

CALVIN IN HIS LETTERS

CALVIN
IN HIS LETTERS

BY

Rev. HENRY F. HENDERSON, M.A.

Author of "Erskine of Linlathen"
"The Religious Controversies of Scotland," etc.

Eugene, Oregon

Wipf and Stock Publishers
199 W 8th Ave, Suite 3
Eugene, OR 97401

Calvin in His Letters
By Henderson, Henry F.
ISBN: 1-57910-008-2
Publication date 11/26/1996
Previously published by J. M. Dent & Company, 1909

FOREWORD

THERE can be no doubt that Calvin regarded *The Institutes* as his masterpiece, his *magnum opus.* A few years before his death, writing to a friend, he says that it "holds the principal and far most conspicuous place among all my lucubrations." And yet if we wish to see the man at his best, and as he lived his life of wonderful activity and fruitfulness, we must turn our attention to his correspondence. There we find ourselves brought into contact with one of the most remarkable personalities in history, and getting at a knowledge of the man, we come to have a better appreciation of his work. His letters also supply abundant means for repairing the damage done to his reputation by the persistent association of his name with certain dark deeds and still darker dogmas.

CONTENTS

CALVIN IN HIS LETTERS

OUTLINE OF LIFE

We begin our study of *Calvin* as seen *in his Letters* by recalling to the reader's mind the principal events in his life. John Calvin was born in Noyon, Picardy, on July 10, 1509. He was the second son of Gérard Cauvin or Calvin and of Jeanne le Franc, his wife. Gérard, who held sundry legal offices under the Church, was a respected member of the community. "I had a somewhat severe father," said his celebrated son, "and I rejoice at it as the source of any virtues which I may possess." His mother was distinguished for religious devotion and for her remarkable beauty. The ecclesiastical lawyer was in a position to rear his children in comfort and give them a good education. John attended school in Paris with a nobleman's family from the district, and easily outstripped all his schoolfellows.

John Calvin was intended by his father to be educated for the priesthood. Accordingly, when he was but twelve years old he received through his father's influence the chaplaincy of La Gesine of the Holy Virgin in the Noyon Cathedral, and six years later he obtained in like manner the living of St. Martin de Marteville. A deputy, of course, performed the duties of these offices, but the holder of them drew the emoluments. To our way of thinking this was nothing else than a church scandal, but at the time it was thought no more of than for a parent to-day to use his influence to obtain a scholarship or exhibition for his son. John was never ordained to the priesthood, and when personal religion took possession of him in his twenty-third year, he resigned his benefices.

The father altered his mind with regard to a profession for his son, and resolved to make him a lawyer. In deference to his wishes, therefore, John, in 1527, became a law student in the University of Orleans. When he left the university, in token of his distinguished merits, he was awarded the highest honours of the Faculty without requiring to pay the customary fees. In 1531 he was attracted to the University of Bourges by the fame of Andrew Alciat, the celebrated jurist. At that place he formed the friendship of Melchior Wolmar, and from that distinguished scholar he acquired a knowledge of the Greek language. His father dying that year, John abandoned the study of law, but his legal training stood him in good service when he became the spiritual ruler of Geneva.

In 1532 we find him in Paris superintending the education of his younger brother Anthony. The same year he embarked on his first literary venture—a commentary on Seneca's *De Clementia.* Some have credited him with polemical motives in this composition, and have regarded the commentary as intended for the benefit of Francis I., the then ruler of France, to remind the monarch, as Seneca sought to remind Nero, how insecurely a tyrant sits upon his throne. But probably Calvin had no such intentions, being attracted to the subject by a scholar's love of literature and a profound admiration for the noble-minded Stoic. In a letter to Francis Daniel, a companion of his youth, he betrays the young author's anxiety for the sale of his book. "My commentaries on the books of Seneca have been printed, but at my own expense, and have drawn from me more money than you can well suppose. At present I am using every endeavour to collect some of it back. I have stirred up some of the professors of this city to make use of them in learning. In the University of Bourges I have induced a friend to do this from the pulpit by a public lecture. You can also help me not a little if you will not take it amiss: you will do so on the score of our old friendship; especially as without any damage to your reputation you may do me this service, which will also tend perhaps to the public good. Should you determine to oblige me by this benefit, I will send you 100 copies, or as many as you please. Meanwhile accept this copy for yourself, while you are not to suppose that by your acceptance of it I hold you engaged to do what I ask. It is my wish that all may be free and unconstrained between us."

Somewhere about 1533 a great spiritual change came over him, regarding which, however, he seems to have been studiously reserved. But from this time onward he identified himself with the Reformed party in Paris and elsewhere. Nicolas Cop, one of his personal friends, was then Rector of Paris University. It fell to the rector to deliver an oration annually in presence of the professors and students at the Feast of All Saints in the beginning of November. John Calvin, it is said, had a hand in the composition of the oration for the year, and as it contained many bold expressions in condemnation of the corruptions of the church, it caused a considerable furor. To escape the blaze they had kindled, Cop and he had to flee from the capital for the time, and occupy themselves in the seclusion of the country. There were not wanting far-seeing persons who now said, "Calvin will be a distinguished instrument in restoring the Kingdom of God in France."

In 1534 he returned to Paris and met for the first time—would that it had been for the last time!—the Spaniard, Michael Servetus. Servetus, though a clever man and one far in advance of his age, was all the same something of a braggadocio. Hearing of Calvin's fame as a disputant and friend of the Reformation, and desirous of airing his own peculiar views on the subject of the Holy Trinity, he invited Calvin to meet him for the purpose of discussion. The latter readily accepted the challenge, but Servetus failed to keep his engagement, and the meeting never took place. "How easily," remarks one of Calvin's biographers, "might a friendly conversation have united these two men in the bonds of amity!"

Religious literature now received from Calvin his first contribution in a work directed not against the Papacy, but against an Anabaptist heresy, the notion that the human soul at the hour of death either perishes with the body, or enters on a state of slumber, in which it continues, without memory, or intelligence, or sensation till the day of judgment. The work was dated from Orleans, 1534, and bore the title *Psychopannychia, qua refellitur quorundam imperitorum error, qui animas post mortem usque ad ultimum judicium dormire putant.* In repelling the Anabaptist doctrine Calvin adopted that attitude of submission to the authority of Holy Scripture which characterised him to the last. "I know," he said, "what power novelty has to tickle the ears of men, but we ought to remember that there is but one word of Life, that which proceeds from the mouth of the Lord. To this alone we should open our ears so far as the doctrine of salvation is concerned and shut them to every other. His Word is not new, but was from the beginning, and will remain. As those are in an error who stigmatise as a novelty the Word of God when brought to light after it had long lain neglected through slothfulness and perverse custom, so they also err, on the other hand, who are like reeds shaken by the wind; nay, bend and turn with every breath. Is this to learn Christ—to listen to any doctrine which may be taught without perceiving a foundation for it in the Word of God?"

In 1536, in the congenial literary atmosphere of Basel, his greatest intellectual achievement came to the birth. Here he brought forth the monumental work, *Christianae Religionis Institutio*. It came out without the author's name, and was dedicated to Francis I. in one of the noblest addresses that were ever penned. What moved him to write was his desire to refute the calumnies with which those professing the Reformed religion were continually assailed. "I am not afraid to confess," he said to Francis, "that I present you with a summary of that doctrine which, if the vociferations of its enemies are to be believed, ought to be punished with imprisonment, banishment, confiscation, and the stake, and to be exterminated by sea and land. I know well with what atrocious informations they fill your ears, to make our cause odious to you; but it becomes you in your clemency to consider that if it is sufficient to accuse, there can be no innocency in words or actions. That we do not make this complaint without reason, you yourself, most noble King, can witness, before whom we are daily traduced and calumniated, as persons who wish to wrest the sceptre from the hands of kings, to overthrow all tribunals and seats of justice, subvert all order and government, disturb the public peace, abolish all laws, dissipate every kind of heritage and property—in fine, turn all things upside down." Twenty-one years later he found it necessary to send a written confession of the Protestant faith in a letter to Francis's successor, Henry II., in order to refute certain calumnious charges—of a similar kind—under which it again lay.[1]

After paying a visit to the court of the Duchess of Ferrara, the accomplished daughter of Louis XII. of France, and a warm supporter of the Reformation faith, a journey which he made under the assumed name of M. Charles d'Espeville, he travelled to Noyon, where he was engaged for a brief time in certain family affairs. Thereafter he landed in Geneva, July 1536. At Geneva he only intended to stay for a night, purposing to make Basel or Strassburg his home during the then troubled state of France, and settling down to a life of study. But William Farel, the Reformer, was in Geneva when he arrived, and he commanded Calvin in the name of Christ to remain with him and help him in the work of God.

[1] Bonnet, Letter 480.

Farel would take no refusal, and went as far as to imprecate on Calvin and his studies the curse of God should he make them his excuse for declining the call. At Geneva, therefore, Calvin remained with Farel for the next two years, and was employed, first, in the capacity of a theological lecturer in the cathedral, and afterwards as one of the regular city clergy. The moral condition of the city—reformed indeed, but not transformed—can be guessed from a remark of Beza's. " Popery," he says, " had indeed been forsworn, but many had not cast away with it those numerous and disgraceful disorders which had for a long time flourished in the city, given up as it was for so many years to canons and impure priests." In a heroic endeavour to cope with " those numerous and disgraceful disorders," of which Beza speaks, Farel and his young colleague prepared articles for the government of the church, laid them before the ordinary council, and had them approved of both by that council and by the Council of the Two Hundred. Among other things it was provided by these articles that the Lord's Supper should be celebrated four times a year; that baptism should be administered on any day when there was a public congregation, and that marriages should also be celebrated in public after the proclamation of banns on three successive Sundays. Provision also was to be made for the clergy; all shops were to be closed on the Lord's Day during sermon; images were to be removed; licentiousness and gambling to be punished. This seems a mild programme of reform, but it proved too rigid for the easy morals of the Genoese. "Have we put down a Papal tyranny only to set up a Protestant one in its place?" they asked. Murmuring grew to rebellion, and at length, under the influence of popular agitation, the Council of the Two Hundred, two years after Calvin's coming among them, pronounced sentence of banishment on Farel and him. Calvin took his punishment philosophically. "Had I been the servant of man I should have received but poor wages," he said to the council, "but happy for me it is that I am the servant of Him who never fails to give His servants that which He has promised them."

Calvin found pleasant refuge in Strassburg, from his time of exile in September 1538, till his return to Geneva in September 1541. One of his college friends, now a young Romish priest, offered him money. "It is possible you may be ill provided with money, without which," he wrote, " you cannot live in a manner becoming you; but you need not mind about that, I will supply enough to meet your necessity." Calvin felt deeply touched by the man's kindness, but with characteristic independence gratefully declined the helping hand. The years that he spent in Strassburg were happy and fruitful. He enjoyed the respect of the citizens, received from the magistrates the rights of citizenship, and became a centre of attraction for students and men of learning. During his sojourn in Strassburg, not only was he able to perform many important services to the Reformation cause, but his own higher nature experienced a remarkable growth and development. By his efforts a French Reformed congregation was set up, and he became its pastor. While exercising his ministry in Strassburg, he delivered courses of lectures in theology, wrote his famous letter to Cardinal Sadolet, enlarged, corrected, and completed the *Institutio*, and composed the first of his great exegetical works. From Strassburg, too, he attended several Imperial Conferences at Ratisbon and elsewhere, became acquainted with Philip Melanchthon—an acquaintanceship which may have cooled[1] somewhat towards the close,

[1] Bonnet, Letter 465.

but for long was warm and mutually helpful—and by travel and social intercourse enlarged his mental horizon and enriched his feelings of sympathy. He even found time, during this period of exile, to take to himself a wife, and with Idelette de Bure he lived in happy wedlock till her decease in 1549.

In 1541 he returned to Geneva and laboured in it for its good during the last twenty-three years of his life. To consent to return to it was a task which he found extremely difficult. Time and again he received pressing invitations to return and let the past be forgotten, and while he sometimes felt himself urged from within to accept the olive branch of peace, he had a horror of facing the ungrateful Genevese. "There is no place," he told Viret, "under heaven of which I can have a greater dread, not because I have hated it, but because I see so many difficulties presented in that quarter which I do feel myself far from being able to surmount," and yet he added, "I cannot tell how it happens, I begin to feel more of an inclination to take the helm in hand should circumstances so require." That the Council of the Two Hundred, by whose sentence he had been banished, should now assemble and unanimously request his return, could not but weigh with him. They had met, and without one dissentient voice they cried, "We must have Calvin, that wise and holy man, that faithful minister of Christ." What could he do but return?

His life was not a prolonged one—he died at the age of fifty-five—but he lived long enough to see his influence dominant at Geneva. It was a long and a hard fight, however. What he suffered from the rude and dissolute libertines made him aged: the taunts hurled at him by friends bowed him down with grief. "The preachers of the Bernese territory denounce me for a heretic," he complains to Bullinger,[1] and it smote him mortally to think that there could be "wicked calumniators, who from the pulpit, in market places, in cross-ways, and at dinner-parties, revile me as a pestilent heretic."[2] But he ultimately triumphed over all difficulties, and before his death in 1564 he had the satisfaction of knowing that while he found Geneva a disorderly Alpine city, he left it "a fair metropolis of the human mind."

What he did for the world and for after generations by his legacies of sacred learning, as also how profoundly his spirit and doctrines have

[1] Bonnet, Letter 365. [2] *Ibid.*, Letter 396.

influenced nations and churches in the old world and the new, cannot be dealt with here in a bare outline of his life. Nor need we pronounce judgment upon the Servetus tragedy further than to say in the words of Professor Walker that "to understand the case of Servetus and its effects on Calvin's fortunes as well as Calvin's attitude toward it, one must so far as possible divest oneself of the prejudgments which three centuries and a half of progress in religious freedom since that time have engendered, and try to look upon it from the common view-point of the sixteenth century." [1]

His farewell words to the Genevese ministers a month before his death are those of one to whom life has been a noble trust: "When I first came to this church it had well-nigh nothing. There was preaching and that is all. The idols were sought out and burned; but there was no reformation. All was in confusion. I have lived in marvellous combats here. I have been saluted in mockery of an evening by fifty or sixty gun-shots before my door. Fancy how that could shock a poor student, timid as I am, and as I confess I have always been. As concerns my doctrine: I have taught faithfully and God has

[1] *John Calvin*, 325.

given me grace to write. I have done it with the utmost fidelity and have not, to my knowledge, corrupted or twisted a single passage of the Scriptures: and when I could have drawn out a far-fetched meaning, if I had studied subtility, I have put that underfoot, and have always studied simplicity. I have written nothing through hatred against any one, but have always set before me faithfully what I have thought to be for the glory of God."

CHAPTER I

THE CORRESPONDENT

A MAN'S letters generally reveal something regarding his character that would otherwise never be known. But for a sentence here and there in his correspondence, who would ever have believed Claverhouse capable of showing humane consideration towards a Covenanting prisoner? So with John Calvin. In his pulpit of the Cathedral of St. Peter, in the Consistory and Council Chambers, in his *Institutes*, Calvin does not draw us by the force of an attractive personality. On the contrary, he awes and repels us. His teaching seems so forbidding, some of his public acts are so barbarous. But in his letters we see a better side of his nature, and get to understand some things about his public work which helps to reconcile us to it. In his letters, it is like seeing him face to face, and speaking to him as a man speaks to his friend. In a few minutes of this close and intimate intercourse, we learn more about the man and his strange life and opinions than by long study of his books.

Great letter-writers, it has been truly said,

have usually been men who have received some mortal wound that has forced them into retirement from the field of battle. It was not so with John Calvin, however. He was a great letter-writer, and yet was on active duty up to the last. His days were incredibly full. Any day might find him in the early hours writing at his commentaries, later preaching the daily sermon in the cathedral, next delivering a lecture in the Academy, then sitting in council settling some church dispute, in addition to which he might receive a dozen callers on business at his house, and end up the day by writing four long friendly letters that will probably prove the most lasting thing he did. Whatever impression we may form of his public life and his ideals, we cannot but be mentally quickened and toned up in the company of one who is such a marvel of keen and many-sided activity.

Calvin had a desire that his letters should be collected and preserved. It is said that, a few days before his death, pointing with failing hands to a pile of manuscript on the floor, he expressed the wish that some friend might gather up the letters written by and to him and make a present of the collection to the Reformed churches. This duty was worthily fulfilled by his own secretary,

Charles de Jonvillers. He devoted twenty years of his life to the arduous task of searching for the precious documents and afterwards transcribing them. The labour involved him in many a long and expensive journey. The volume which he compiled formed the foundation of the enormous collection of correspondence—much of it still unpublished—in the Library of Geneva.

The letters deal with an astonishing variety of topics. Usually, of course, the grave and momentous concerns of religion and church rule engage the writer's attention, and for the most part they are addressed to important personages, reformation leaders in other lands, statesmen and men of affairs, sometimes even to crowned heads. At other times they are the outpourings of love and good-will, soundings of the heart, from one friend to another. At times, the bow is unstrung and the writer abandons himself to trivial matters in the racy style. On these rare occasions we remember that Calvin is a Frenchman. What could be in happier vein than his plans for a week in the country with his friend Viret? "When some one or other informed me lately that you intended coming here in a short time, I snatched eagerly at the intelligence, just as if you had been bound to come by a previous agreement. If you do think of coming, I beseech you, again and again, to stay a Sabbath with us, for you could not have a better opportunity during the whole year. You will deliver a discourse in the city on the morning of the Lord's Day. I shall set out for Jussy: you will follow me after dinner, and we shall proceed thence to M. de Falais" (a great friend of Calvin's who had a country-seat a few leagues from Geneva). "Leaving him again, we shall make a hasty passage to the opposite side" (the other side of the lake), "and rusticate till Thursday with Seigneurs Pommier and De Lisle. On Friday, if you choose to make an excursion to Tournet or Belle Rive, you will have my company also. You need not be afraid of any unpopularity, for matters have calmed down somewhat, as you will hear. See you do not disappoint me. Certainly many here are expecting you."[1]

Take again his free and easy account of life in Geneva lodgings, and how he comported himself through a small domestic pickle. "On the Monday," he writes to Farel, "a circumstance occurred which had provoked my anger: for when the housekeeper, as oft she does, spoke more freely than became her, and had addressed

[1] Bonnet, Letter 264.

some rude expressions to my brother, he could not brook her impertinence, not, however, that he made any stir about it, but he silently left the house, and vowed solemnly that he would not return so long as she remained with me. Therefore, when she saw me so sad on account of my brother's departure, she also went elsewhere. Her son, in the meanwhile, continued to live with me. I am wont, however, when heated by anger, or stirred up by some greater anxiety than usual, to eat to excess, and to devour my meat more eagerly than I ought, which so happened to me at that time. Whenever the stomach is oppressed overnight with too much, or with unsuitable food, I am tormented in the morning with severe indigestion. To correct that by fasting was a ready cure, and that was my usual practice; but in order that the son of our housekeeper might not interpret this abstinence to be an indirect way of getting rid of him, I rather chose, at the expense of health, not to incur that offence."[1] What an accommodating man!

From this example of the ludicrous, let us pass to an example of the sublime. It is a letter of consolation to a gentleman on the death of his son. The writer is at Ratisbon, attending the

[1] Bonnet, Letter 52.

Conference, and although he has not a moment's leisure there, he finds time to write in choice language and at great fulness to the bereaved father: "When I first received the intelligence, I was so utterly overpowered that for many days I was fit for nothing but to grieve; and albeit I was somehow upheld before the Lord by those aids wherewith He sustains our souls in affliction, among men, however, I was a nonentity: so far at least as regards my discharge of duty, I appeared to myself quite as unfit for it as if I had been half dead. There is most assuredly one sure and certain, a never-failing source of consolation, in which you and men like you ought to acquiesce, because it flows from that inward feeling of piety which I know to abound in you: therefore take special care to call to mind those thoughts which are taught us by the most excellent Master of all, and suggested to our understanding in the school of piety. In what regards your son, if you bethink yourself how difficult it is, in this most deplorable age, to maintain an upright course through life, you will judge him to be blessed, who, before encountering so many coming dangers which already were hovering over him and to be encountered in his day and generation, was so early delivered from them all.

He is like one who has set sail upon a stormy and tempestuous sea, and before he has been carried out into the deeps, gets in safely to the secure haven." [1]

Calvin's correspondence is impressive on account of its copiousness and variety, the light it throws on the writer's character, and the information it supplies regarding the great work in which he engaged. It furnishes also not a little food for wonder when we consider the extraordinary difficulties that must have attended the conveyance of letters in olden times. Accustomed as we are to the facilities and conveniences of the modern postal system, we simply do not realise the trouble and the expenditure which the delivery of letters in Calvin's time involved. Most of his correspondents were at a considerable distance from where he wrote, many of them resided in foreign states and in localities not easy of access. The wonder is that, after having written his letters, he ever got them delivered at their destination at all! In ordinary circumstances, a special courier had to be employed, and that meant a good deal of expense. Horses as well as men had to be engaged that were fit and trustworthy for their work. Frequently

[1] Bonnet, Letter 64.

the unsafe condition of the roads, and the many accidents to which travellers were exposed rendered the business of conveyance precarious and perilous in the extreme. It need not surprise us to hear that occasionally the most valuable documents went amissing through the fault or misfortune of those bearing them from place to place. Sometimes when a letter was all ready for despatch, it lay on Calvin's desk for ten days waiting for a proper messenger. He mentions one that came to him "crushed and rumpled with much rough usage, having been kept four months in the messenger's hand." On another occasion he describes the courier who is bearing his letter as "a worker in gold, but a fellow who is deserving of the gallows." At another time he has to complain that his letter had been broken open on the way. To a friend he confesses that he would oftener have written to him, if a messenger could have been had to carry the letters. When he wrote to the King of England and to Somerset, the Protector, the bearer of his letters was his own faithful servant Nicolas. Nicolas was detained eleven days "by head winds, and afterwards tossed about by so severe tempests that he scarcely escaped shipwreck."

Another cause for wonder is that with the

huge tasks they set before them, the volumes they wrote, the sermons and lectures they delivered sometimes daily, their preparation of catechisms, creeds, and prayer-books, their attendance at courts and diets, the Reformers had time for letter-writing at all. Yet they all wrote hundreds of letters. It seems to have been a joy and a relaxation to them in the midst of their strenuous labours. It was so to Calvin. "Had I only to write to you," he says to his friend M. de Falais, "it would be to me a very easy labour, if that can be called toil wherein one only finds pleasure." [1]

Men of the most different characters were among Calvin's correspondents. Perhaps there could not have been two more unlike than Cranmer and Socinus. Cranmer has evidently a warm place in Calvin's heart. He writes to him about his work as Tennyson praises him for his goodness—

> "To do him any wrong
> Was to beget a kindness from him, for his heart was rich:
> Of such fine mould that if you sowed therein
> The seeds of hate, it blossomed charity."

Calvin writes: "Especially most illustrious archbishop, is it necessary for you, in proportion to the dignified position you occupy, to turn

[1] Bonnet, Letter 161.

your attention as you are doing to this object" (the union of the Reformed churches). "I do not say this as if to spur you on to greater exertions, who are not only of your own accord in advance of others, but are also, as a voluntary encourager, urging them on: I say it in order that by my congratulations you may be strengthened in a pursuit so auspicious and noble."[1]

It is in a different tone he writes to Socinus. In a paternal fashion, as Dr. Chalmers would have written to Edward Irving, apprehensive of the young man's intellectual vagaries, and perhaps not succeeding very well in understanding the young man's point of view, Calvin says: "I am very greatly grieved that the fine talents with which God has endowed you should be occupied not only with what is vain and fruitless, but that they should also be injured by pernicious figments. What I warned you of long ago, I must again seriously repeat, that unless you correct in time this itching after investigation, it is to be feared you will bring upon yourself severe suffering. Adieu, brother, very highly esteemed by me: and if this rebuke is harsher than it ought to be, ascribe it to my love for you."[2]

[1] Bonnet, Letter 293. [2] *Ibid.*, Letter 288.

CHAPTER II

THE MAN

One is apt to think of Calvin as an unlovable and unsympathetic man. We associate him in our minds with hard and gloomy theological ideas. But let us look at the man as he is revealed in his letters. Besides the stern and unyielding figure that repels and alarms us, there is a Calvin who wins us by his large-hearted humanity, and even by his betrayal of attractive human weaknesses. For instance, he could no more be discourteous to a lady than any other Frenchman. Thus, on a certain occasion of which he speaks in one of his letters, when he did not desire to avail himself of a lady's kind attentions to him, we find him resorting like any ordinary man of the world to a harmless subterfuge. Writing to his friend Farel, he tells him: "The Lady R. at first invited me thither; but because the way did not appear sufficiently open I excused myself on the ground of being detained here by another engagement, which was indeed a small matter, but quite sufficient to lay me under the obligation of attending to it."[1] Cal-

[1] Bonnet, Letter 32.

vin, whatever else he was or was not, does not, judging from this extract, appear to have been one of your uncomfortably over-rigid people.

He had not Luther's vein of satire that was so sharp and witty, but, when occasion called for it, his sarcasm was often like a rapier thrust. The answer that he gave to those who taunted him with making a fine thing out of it by his position in Geneva is a good specimen of his capacity for raillery. He said he wished that his critics might be appointed his successors!

When he would induce his friend M. de Falais to come to Geneva and take up his abode there, he slyly adds that he has laid in a cask of good wine for his benefit. "I wish very much that it may please God to bring you hither to drink of the wine upon the spot and that soon. If the bearer had left this earlier in the morning, you might have had a flask of it. If there were any means of sending you the half of it, I should not have failed to do so, but when I inquired, I found that it could not be done."[1] Calvin, we see, had some very human traits.

Like other men of genius, he took himself seriously, and had a lofty sense of his importance in the universe. This comes out in one of his

[1] Bonnet, Letter 225.

letters to that friend whom he loved almost more than all others, Philip Melanchthon: "I know and confess, moreover, that we occupy widely different positions; still, because I am not ignorant of the place in His theatre to which God has elevated me, there is no reason for my concealing that our friendship could not be interrupted without great injury to the church."[1]

Was he blind to the beauty of the natural world? It has been said that though living by the Lake of Geneva, and in sight of Mont Blanc, he apparently had no eye for the grand and the beautiful in nature. Perhaps. I rather think, however, that rural retirement appealed to him, and probably also the pleasures of a garden. At least in his correspondence with M. de Falais about a house in Geneva, there is something that seems to point in that direction. It is curious, by the way, to find him well informed in all the details of house-hunting and negotiations with landlords. The extract which follows is long, but it shows us the great theologian in such an interesting light that to shorten it would be to spoil it. "As for yourself, in obedience to the commission which you gave me, I have looked about since my return for a convenient lodging.

[1] Bonnet, Letter 304.

As for that of Clébergue, you would be too far away from the neighbours you desire, although I have long had a wish for it myself, for the sake of retirement, when I seek to have leisure; and they promised to let me have an answer, but none has come. If I had it at my disposal, as they had given me to hope, you know that it would be very much at your service. Near us, I have not been able to find one having a garden which would be more suitable for you than the one which I have taken. Not that I am quite content with the lodging, but I took it for want of a better. You will have in front a small garden and a tolerably spacious court. Behind there is another garden. A great saloon with as beautiful a view as you could desire for the summer. The other rooms have not so pleasant an aspect as I would like. But when you have arrived, possibly we may devise some satisfactory arrangement. With the exception of the saloon one might find houses better furnished and more conveniently laid out; but there would have been no garden, and I see that is a feature which you desire above all. However that may be, it is hired for twelve crowns. When you see it, if you say that this is too much, I shall have my excuse ready, that I am not such a manager as to be very sparing of my purse, any more than of that of others. I have hurried on the bargain solely on account of the garden. If time hangs heavy with you where you are, it appears to me the season will be as suitable in a month as at a later period, provided that the weather be as favourable as it usually is at that time. As for escort, although my brother is not here at this moment, I can safely venture to undertake for him that he will willingly serve you; and he has gone that road so often that he ought to know it well. Moreover, he has already had to do with the boatmen; and I believe you will recollect my advice, that you should come part of the way by water, to refresh you. Awaiting your full resolve, we shall sow without making any stir about it, and prune the vines." [1]

M. de Falais discovers that should he elect to reside in Geneva, he will be in danger of losing his rights and privileges as a burgess of Basel. Calvin takes up the matter and talks like a family lawyer to his friend: "I had not thought that you would need expressly to renounce your rights as a burgess, although I foresaw clearly that it would amount to a tacit renunciation when you settled your domicile in another seigneury." [2]

[1] Bonnet, Letter 186 (*conf.* Letter 381). [2] *Ibid.*, Letter 219.

Calvin was thus, we see, a man, and nothing human was uninteresting to him. Even at the time when he was busy corresponding with the English Protector, Somerset, as to the best method of advancing the truth in England, we find him actually writing to Farel about a domestic-servant difficulty in which the latter was involved. "I understand that you require a maid-servant —neither yourself nor your brothers told me so. However, having heard it from others, I wish to tell you that there is a woman here, who is pious, upright, and careful, and advanced in years, who would gladly serve you if she could be of use to you."[1] I wonder if there was any kind of human service to which this man was not ready to put his hand. We shall yet see him in negotiations of a far more difficult and delicate character than finding Farel a housekeeper.

We have already cited an example of Calvin's self-consciousness. The belief never departed from him—a belief which he shared in common with all the pilots of the race and pioneers of progress—that he occupied a considerable rank in the army of Divine Providence, and was a divinely-appointed instrument in the fulfilment of the will of the Almighty. And yet, personally,

[1] Bonnet, Letter 258.

he seems to have been the most modest of men and one devoid of all pride of intellect. Hear the humble estimate he expresses about himself at the time when the deputies came to him from Geneva, urging him to return to the city that had cast him out, but now needed him and repented of her error. "A horseman," he writes to Farel, "was sent forward, post-haste, to intimate to us that they were on their way. The post preceded them by two days. To their deputies here, however, the council gave direction to do their endeavour so as to prevent my making any promise. Never had I believed that our council set so much value by me. Nor did those who were present read their letter without astonishment at their being so anxious about retaining me, to whom I appeared to be so little known. But mayhap they did so because they were not well enough acquainted with me. For what is there in me to recommend me?"[1] Calvin was never elated over his literary accomplishments. The ideal he aimed at was higher than other men's; and therefore he could not rest and be thankful with what he accomplished. Writing to Farel he says: "My *Antidote*"—a work directed against the decrees of the Council of

[1] Bonnet, Letter 56.

Trent—"now begins to please me, since it is so greatly approved of by you, for before, I was not satisfied with it. But you who know my daily labours, and still more the contests with which I am not so much occupied as quite wasted, are perhaps ready to excuse me when there is anything not quite perfect. I certainly marvel that any composition worthy of perusal can emanate from me." [1]

Let us look at another fine quality in Calvin. We know that many of those who have been proud to call themselves by his name have been sticklers for the veriest trifles, and have separated from one another over theological needle-points. The master, however, was no petty quibbler. Confronted day after day with so many real evils, he could not understand men contending about shows and semblances of evil. Learning that dissension was arising over some ceremonial detail in the celebration of the Lord's Supper, he writes to Farel: "I entreat of you, my dear brother, in so great iniquity of the time in which we live, that you will use your utmost endeavour to keep together all who are any way bearable. As to the trifling ceremonies, strive to induce the brethren not to dispute the point with those of

[1] Bonnet, Letter 214.

their neighbourhood with so much of stiff-necked obstinacy."[1] Would that religious controversialists had ever been of Calvin's sane and sober way of thinking! There were some in his day who disliked Luther because he still cleaved to Popish observances; and they emphasised the things in which they differed from him rather than those in which they were at one. Calvin had no sympathy for such a narrow view. "I wish," he writes to Farel, "that our excellent friend N. could behold how much sincerity there is in Philip. All suspicion of double-dealing would entirely vanish. Besides, as to Bucer's defence of Luther's ceremonies, he does not do so because he eagerly seeks them, or would endeavour to introduce them. By no means can he be brought to approve of chanting in Latin. Images he abhors. Some other things he despises, while others he cares nothing at all about. There is no occasion to fear that he would be for restoring those things which have been once abolished; only he cannot endure that on account of these trifling observances, we should be separated from Luther. Neither, certainly, do I consider them to be just causes of dissent."[2]

[1] Bonnet, Letter 28 (*vid.* Letters 346, 380).
[2] *Ibid.*, Letter 35.

Some of the English Protestants were, according to Calvin, needlessly obstinate on the subject of Popish custom and ceremony. Hooper, for instance, on his consecration to the see of Gloucester, would not clothe himself in the sacerdotal uniform then in vogue on such high occasions. His obstinacy was punished with imprisonment. Calvin, on his watch-tower at Geneva, had his eye on all such happenings in London and elsewhere. It offended Calvin's just sense of proportion to hear of Hooper's position on a matter of mere externals. Writing to Bullinger, he says: "We have heard the sad news of Hooper's imprisonment. I was somewhat apprehensive of this long ago. I am now afraid that the bishops, as if victorious, will become much more ferociously insolent. While, therefore, I admire his firmness in refusing the anointing, I had rather he had not carried his opposition so far with respect to the cap and the linen vestment, even although I do not approve of these."[1] When there was much contention over the words, "this is my body," Calvin wrote to a theological friend: "May the Lord, by His Spirit, dispose us all to true moderation." One never thinks of associating the noble quality of

[1] Bonnet, Letter 275.

moderation with John Calvin, however we may associate it with Leighton and the late Dean Stanley. Surely Calvin has been a misunderstood man.[1]

Calvin was not known in his day as the friend of moderation and large views. The ordinary citizen of Geneva probably regarded him as the impersonation of bigotry, intolerance, severity, and even cruelty. And it is just possible that while Calvin criticised Hooper from a distance quite dispassionately, moderate men in Geneva passed the same condemnation on Calvin and his consistorial court for similar sins at home. All the same, he has been a better exponent of sane and tolerant principles of controversy than he has ever received credit for.

Finer even than his praise of moderation was his noble self-effacement. We have a splendid illustration of this great virtue in his declaration regarding the work of the ministers who superseded him during his enforced absence from Geneva. All his friends regarded them as unworthy and evil-disposed men, but he said with a rare charitableness, " I do not care by whom it is that the work of the Lord is carried forward, provided that it is well done." Such complete

[1] *Vid.* Letter 601.

immunity from reproachful temper towards men who were profiting by his exile stamps our hero as every inch of him a true Christian. It reminds us of the noble sentiments expressed by Browning in "Paracelsus"—

> Lo, I forget my ruin, and rejoice
> In thy success as thou! Let our God's praise
> Go bravely through the world at last. What care
> Through me or thee?

CHAPTER III

THE THEOLOGIAN

NEVER was title better deserved than that which Melanchthon bestowed on Calvin at Ratisbon in 1541. At the Imperial Diet which assembled there in that year, Calvin so greatly distinguished himself beyond all others that his friend named him *the Theologian*. His intellectual powers had ripened early, his great work, *The Institutes of the Christian Religion* having been composed by him at the age of twenty-six. The first edition appeared in Latin in 1536, and was a briefer and in some respects an inferior production to the later editions in 1539 and 1559. In 1541 followed a French edition, translated by himself and intended for the benefit of his fellow-countrymen. Never, as long as he lived, did Calvin alter his beliefs and theological views as set forth at length in *The Institutes*. He drew nothing back. What he had written, he had written. " I leave you to judge," says Scaliger, " whether he was not a great man."

I. In the construction of his colossal system

Calvin took the Apostles' Creed as his ground plan, treating in the first and second books of the knowledge of God as Creator and as Redeemer, in the third of God as Sanctifier, or the doctrine of the Holy Ghost, and in the last of the church, the sacraments, and civil government. What led him to compose this work is well told in his own words: "While I lay concealed in Basel, the burning of so many pious men in France gave great offence throughout Germany, and to allay this feeling certain false and wicked libels were spread, bearing that those who had met with such cruel treatment were Anabaptists and turbulent men who, by their frantic notions, sought to overturn both religious and civil polity. Perceiving that these slanders originated in the artifices of the court, and were calculated not only to bury the blood of the innocent and holy martyrs under a load of infamy, but also to give a licence to commit similar atrocities, without check, for the future, I could not keep silence nor acquit myself from the charge of treachery unless I did all in my power to put a stop to that course of fraud and violence. This was the reason of my publishing *The Institution.* What I then published was not the large work which is now known by the same name, but a small manual; nor did I court fame by it, as is evident from my quitting the place soon after its appearance, and the circumstance that no one then knew that I was the author. This I also concealed elsewhere, and it was my wish to have kept the secret."[1]

One need not be afraid of tackling this book. It is never dull, and at times it is positively lively and entertaining. Calvin can even tell a good story. Speaking of the necessity for a divine revelation, he relates how Simonides, being asked by Hiero the tyrant what God was, requested a day to consider the matter. The tyrant next day repeated the question, but Simonides begged to be allowed two days longer to prepare his answer. Time after time the question is put, and time after time Simonides requests to be allowed to double the number of days for the consideration of the subject. At length he has to confess "the longer I consider the subject, the more obscure it appears to me."[2]

Calvin brushes aside the question as to why God deferred the creation of the world so long, as one that is neither wise nor right, and tells the story of a good old man who, when an idle scoffer asked him what God was doing before He

[1] Preface to the Psalms. [2] *Institutes*, I. 5.

created the heavens and the earth, shrewdly replied that He was then making hell for the over-inquisitive![1] Dealing with some whom he calls *anthropomorphites*, or those who suppose the Divine Being to be corporeal because the Bible frequently ascribes to Him ears, eyes, hands, feet, and a mouth, Calvin puts the point in the happiest form: "Who, even of the meanest capacity, understands not that God lisps, as it were, with us, just as nurses are accustomed to speak to infants?"[2] In a chapter on the guidance and teaching of the Scripture, he is again in the happiest vein. "For as persons who are old," he says, "or whose eyes are by any means become dim, if you show them the most beautiful book, though they perceive something written, but can scarcely read two words together, yet by the assistance of spectacles will begin to read distinctly; so the Scripture, collecting in our minds the otherwise confused notions of Deity, dispels the darkness and gives us a clear view of the true God."[3]

On the awful themes of election and reprobation, which Calvin felt called upon to proclaim, though feeling as much repugnance to the latter as other men do, calling it a horrible decree—

[1] *Institutes*, I. 14. [2] *Ibid.*, I. 13. [3] *Ibid.*, I. 6.

decretum quidem horribile fateor—he says: " But though the discussion of predestination may be compared to a dangerous ocean; yet in traversing over it the navigation is safe and serene, and I will also add pleasant, unless any one freely wishes to expose himself to danger. For as those who, in order to gain an assurance of their election, examine into the eternal counsel of God without the Word plunge themselves into a fatal abyss, so they who investigate it in a regular and orderly manner as it is contained in the Word derive from such inquiry the benefit of peculiar consolation." [1]

This terrible decree of reprobation was Calvin's peculiar contribution to theology, for which very few people have cordially thanked him. Others had taught a doctrine of predestination and the absolute sovereignty of God over His universe, but most of them wisely and humanely hesitated to go further. Calvin had the temerity to drive home his logic to its uttermost lengths, and proclaimed not merely a predestination of some to grace, but a foreordination of others to eternal doom. " Predestination we call the eternal decree of God, by which He hath determined in Himself what He would have to become of every indi-

[1] *Institutes*, III. 24.

vidual of mankind. For they are not all created with a similar destiny; but eternal life is foreordained for some, and eternal damnation for others."[1] "We assert that by an eternal and immutable counsel, God hath once for all determined, both whom He would admit to salvation and whom He would condemn to destruction."[2] "Foolish mortals enter into many contentions with God, as though they could arraign Him to plead to their accusations. In the first place, they inquire by what right the Lord is angry with His creatures who had not provoked Him by any previous offence, for that to devote to destruction whom He pleases is more like the caprice of a tyrant than the lawful sentence of a judge; that men have reason therefore to expostulate with God, if they are predestinated to eternal death without any demerit of their own, merely by His sovereign will. If such thoughts ever enter the minds of pious men, they will be sufficiently enabled to break their violence by this one consideration, how exceedingly presumptuous it is only to inquire into the causes of the divine will, which is in fact, and is justly entitled to be, the cause of everything that exists. For if it has any cause, then there must be something

[1] *Institutes*, III. 21. [2] *Ibid.*, III. 21.

antecedent on which it depends, which it is impious to suppose. For the will of God is the highest rule of justice, so that what He wills must be considered just for this very reason, because He wills it." [1]

Calvin's teaching, as it has had to be apologised for ever since his time, did not pass unchallenged even in his own day. In one of his letters he describes a disturbance caused in a church by Jerome Bolsec, once a Carmelite friar but afterwards a Protestant. "There is one Jerome here who, having thrown off the monk's cowl, is become one of those strolling physicians who, by habitual deception and trickery, acquire a degree of impudence which makes them prompt and ready in venturing upon anything whatever. He made an attempt, eight months ago, in a public assembly of our church, to overthrow the doctrine of God's free election. Then indeed the impertinence of the man was regulated by some degree of moderation. He ceased not afterwards to make a noise in all places with the intention of shaking the faith of the simple in this all-important doctrine. For when one of our brethren recently expounded a passage where Christ declares that those who do not hear God's

[1] *Institutes*, III. 23.

words are not of God, this false and worthless wretch rose up and affirmed that men are not saved because they have been elected, but that they are elected because they believe; that no one is condemned at the mere pleasure of God; that those only are condemned who deprive themselves of the election common to all. In dealing with this question, he inveighed against us with a great deal of violent abuse. The chief magistrate of the city, on hearing of the matter, imprisoned him." [1]

Nor was it left to discredited individuals like Bolsec and Trolliet—of whom we hear in a subsequent letter—to flout the "horrible decree" of John Calvin. Even the mild Melanchthon refused to go all the way with his friend, which drew from the latter a letter of expostulation. In his letter Calvin shows a fine spirit. "It increases my anxiety and at the same time my grief to see you in this matter to be almost unlike yourself; for I heard when the whole formula of the agreement of our church with that of Zurich was laid before you, you instantly seized a pen and erased that sentence which cautiously and prudently makes a distinction between the elect and the reprobate. Which procedure, taking

[1] Bonnet, Letter 284.

into consideration the mildness of your disposition, not to mention other characteristics, greatly shocked me. Would that we might have an opportunity of talking over these matters face to face! I am not ignorant of your candour, of your transparent openness and moderation. As for your piety, it is manifest to angels and to the whole world." [1]

While "greatly shocked" at Melanchthon's cavalier conduct, I do not think he expected a ready subscription to his creed from the ordinary church member. Writing to Farel about an applicant for church membership who "hesitated as to predestination," Calvin says that he had received and welcomed the man, and in spite of a suspicion of unsoundness on the doctrine of election he adds: "Unless I am very much deceived, he is a pious, God-fearing man." [2]

The letters of Calvin afford us abundant proof of the profound influence that the belief in predestination exercised upon his own religious life. The fact that a divine hand had mapped out all his life for him made him walk with firm and assured step over the most difficult paths. The call to return to Geneva and take up again his work there filled him with foreboding and gloom,

[1] Bonnet, Letter 304 (*conf.* Letter 359). [2] *Ibid.*, Letter 30.

and yet he could write to the authorities of that city with a confidence that owed its existence to the faith in God that was in him: "Although the charge of administering the government of such a church would be very difficult to me, yet notwithstanding, seeing that I am at the disposal of God and not at my own, I am always ready to employ myself thereto in whatsoever it shall seem good to Him to call me." [1]

When he has to send a message of consolation to a bereaved friend, again he finds a reason for submission in the sovereignty of God. "What the Lord has done we must at the same time consider has not been done rashly, nor by chance, neither from having been impelled from without, but by that determinate counsel, whereby He not only foresees, decrees, and executes nothing but what is just and upright in itself, but also nothing but what is good and wholesome for us. Where justice and good judgment reign paramount, there it is impious to remonstrate." [2]

From the inspiring thought that Divine Wisdom and Love are at the helm of human affairs, he and his comrade Farel are to draw their courage. "It is as you say, my dear Farel. Although we may be severely buffeted hither

[1] Bonnet, Letter 59. [2] *Ibid.*, Letter 64.

and thither by many tempests, yet seeing that a pilot steers the ship in which we sail, who will never allow us to perish even in the midst of shipwrecks, there is no reason why our minds should be overwhelmed with fear and overcome with weariness." [1]

It is a commonplace of history that the Calvinistic doctrine of divine sovereignty has nerved men to courage as no other motive has done. Warriors like the Prince of Orange, who have displayed a wonderful spirit of endurance and have contended, as he did, against the most formidable odds, have been borne up on their heroic course by the belief that they and all men are instruments in the hand of divine omnipotence. "Calvinism," says Lord Morley, "exalted its votaries to a pitch of heroic moral energy that has never been surpassed. They have exhibited an active courage, a cheerful self-restraint, an exalting self-sacrifice that men count among the highest glories of the human conscience."

The strength that lies in Calvinism, which all fair-minded historians are ready to acknowledge, is hardly the work of Calvin, however. He contributed the darker element to the doctrine, as

[1] Bonnet, Letter 320.

we have seen—an element present to the mind of earlier theologians, no doubt, but which they wisely hesitated to formulate in rigid phraseology. But that is not the source of the Calvinistic strength of which we hear so much. Calvinistic belief is strong and capable of producing heroism, not in virtue of what is distinctively Calvinistic in it, but through that which it has in common with all Christian creeds—the belief in a Sovereign Lord of love, wisdom, and omnipotence behind and beside all movements and all men, urging them forward to fulfil His will, and blessing them individually in so far as they are workers together with Him.

Calvin was wont to say[1] that while his name and his writings might be forgotten, what the prophets and the apostles had said would endure for ever, and it was from them he derived his teaching. And yet he was not an infallible interpreter of Scripture, great exegete though he was, especially when his favourite doctrine was involved. He sometimes confounded what Scripture teaches as to the historical destiny of nations and individuals here and now in this world with statements regarding their eternal fate in the world to come. It is also the case that he attached far too little importance to Scripture

[1] Bonnet, Letter 398.

teachings on the other side, like 1 Tim. ii. 4, and 2 Peter iii. 9.

He pushed logical methods too far. In dealing with religious issues we have no right to allow the faculty of reason to override the better feelings of our nature.

We all admit that God has an election of grace, but who has the right to say that such as seem to us to live and die outside this circle have been eternally passed by? In their case, what if the election to grace has been, as Martensen thinks, merely postponed? Whatever be the truth in the matter, Bengel was not far wrong when he said that we should not be too curious to look at God behind the scenes!

II. As an expounder of Scripture, whether we have regard to the quality or to the quantity of his work, Calvin must be pronounced the master exegete of the Reformation period. If Luther had the genius for translating the Scriptures, Calvin had the genius for interpreting them. With the new interest in Biblical learning that came with the Reformation, the Reformers became emulous to shine as Bible expositors. On all hands, even according to bitter theological antagonists, Calvin was declared to have earned the palm. Father Simon, in his day (1638-1712) a learned and famous priest of the Roman Catholic Church, paid him a tribute that was indeed wonderful coming from the quarter it did: "As Calvin was endued with a lofty genius, we are constantly meeting with something in his commentaries which delights the mind; and in consequence of his intimate and perfect acquaintance with human nature, his ethics are truly charming, while he does his utmost to maintain their accordance with the sacred text. Had he been less under the influence of prejudice, and had he not been solicitous to become the leader and standard-bearer of heresy, he might have produced a work of the greatest usefulness to the Catholic Church."

Not less remarkable was the verdict of Arminius, who stands theologically at the opposite pole from Calvin. "Next to the perusal of the Scriptures," he said, "which I earnestly inculcate, I exhort my pupils to peruse Calvin's commentaries." Dr. James Morison, another witness from the opponent's camp, held Calvin's commentaries in high estimation. He repeatedly quotes Calvin in his own work on *Matthew*, and in one page calls him "one of the noblest of uninspired men."

The letters do not furnish much information as regards Calvin's exegetical work. To behold what precious gems the Genevan theologian discovered in the Bible, one would need to enter the house of the interpreter and see for oneself. In the letters we come across some interesting things relative to this branch of his theological work, however.

In one we find Calvin forwarding a copy of his commentary on *Isaiah* and that on the *Canonical Epistles* to King Edward of England, to whom also he dedicated the volumes. "Sire," he begins, "if I must excuse myself towards your Majesty for having used the boldness to dedicate these books which I now present to you, I would need to find an advocate to speak a word for me. For so far would my letter be from having credit enough to do that, that it would even stand in need of a fresh excuse. And, indeed, as I should never have taken upon me to address the commentaries to you which I have published with your name, neither should I have ventured now to write to you, but for the confidence I had already conceived, that both would be well received. For, inasmuch as holding me to be among the number of those who are zealous for the advancement of the kingdom of the Son of

God, you have not disdained to read what I did not specially present to your Majesty, I have thought that if, while serving Jesus Christ my Master, I could likewise testify to the reverence and singular affection which I bear you, I could not fail to find a kind and courteous acceptance."[1]

Calvin was not mistaken in young King Edward. The books were well received. "If I am not deceived," he writes to Farel six months thereafter, "the work not only greatly pleased the Royal Council, but also filled the king himself with extraordinary delight. The Archbishop of Canterbury informed me that I could do nothing more useful than to write to the king more frequently. This gave me more pleasure than if I had come to the possession of a great sum of money."[2]

Calvin dedicated many of his works to European crowned heads. His commentary on the *Hebrews* was dedicated in 1549 to Sigismund Augustus, King of Poland. In 1552 he dedicated the first part of his commentary on *Acts* to Christian I. of Sweden, and in 1554 the second part to his son Frederick. That he should seek to interest the great of the earth in his exposi-

[1] Bonnet, Letter 273. [2] *Ibid.*, Letter 278.

tions of Scripture shows, perhaps, the great importance he attached to such work.

Calvin's output of exegetical work was something amazing. He wrote commentaries on almost the whole of the Old Testament books, and with the exception of one—the book of Revelation—he produced commentaries on every book of the New Testament. He had indeed been well provided for this enormous work. Learning and scholarship came easy to him; and in addition to rich intellectual stores, he had a great knowledge of life, as Father Simon points out, and a vast experience of the human heart. There can be no doubt that the trials and struggles of his public life helped him not a little in the work of Scripture interpretation. He tells us so in the Preface to the Psalms: "Now, if my readers derive any fruit and advantage from the labour which I have bestowed in writing these commentaries, I would have them to understand that the small measure of experience which I have had by the conflicts with which the Lord has exercised me, has in no ordinary degree assisted me, not only in applying to present use whatever instruction could be gathered from these divine compositions, but also in more easily comprehending the design of each of the writers."

It is recorded in the life of Oliver Goldsmith that when asked by a young person to name a good commentary on the Scriptures, the genial man replied that common sense was one of the best commentators he knew. Calvin's sound sense, his sobriety, reasonableness, and practical character are the prominent qualities of his work. On the whole, too, he is free from prejudice and partisanship. Nothing will tempt him "to lie for God." Tholuck singles out his exegetical tact for special praise. "When the interpreter of our times meets with passages in the New Testament or even in the Old, where the common orthodox view gives a sense too rigid and repulsive, let him open Calvin, and he will commonly find this rigid idea developed from the connection in a lively and attractive manner."

III. The letters supply abundant information as to Calvin's middle position on the sacrament controversy. According to him the Lord's Supper was less than Luther's consubstantiation theory made it and more than Zwingli's symbolic theory. In a letter to Bullinger, he makes a clear and instructive statement: "With regard to the sacraments in general, we neither bind up the grace of God with them, nor transfer to them the work or power of the Holy Spirit, nor constitute them the ground of the assurance of salvation. We expressly declare that it is God alone who acts by means of the sacraments, and we maintain that their whole efficacy is due to the Holy Spirit. Nor do we teach that the sacrament is of profit, otherwise than as it leads us by the hand to Christ, that we may seek in Him whatever blessings there are." [1]

[1] Bonnet, Letter 224 (*conf.* Letter 356).

CHAPTER IV

THE PASTOR

A PASTOR'S life in Geneva in the sixteenth century is tolerably well drawn in Calvin's letters, and so far as can be seen, it was not so very different from what ministerial experience is to-day among ourselves. As a young divine, fresh from the lectures of the Academy, he was greatly shocked by the gross ignorance of his congregation in regard to religious matters. "I have not found a single individual in this church," he tells Viret, "who has even a competent understanding of this sacrament."[1] Like other clergymen, too, he was liable to get victimised by impostors. In a letter to his friend Myconius, he describes a character who brought him a tale about being robbed of all his possessions by a highwayman. Calvin lent the man a sum of money, in return for which he left a box in pledge. Not hearing from him again, Calvin opened the box and found it contained mouldy apples! He then returned the box to its owner, who went about the city proclaiming Calvin to be a thief, having broken open his box![2]

[1] Bonnet, Letter 92.

[2] *Ibid.*, Letter 83.

Calvin exercised a faithful minister's care for the poor of his flock. Writing from Worms to his ministerial *locum tenens*, he lets us see that his pastoral anxieties were not left behind when he went on a distant journey. "I am not a little perplexed," he says, "in the devising of a method by which to give assistance to the poor. If only so much shall be found in the poor-box from whence you can supply the present need until my return, we shall then deliberate together what better can be done." [1]

A conscientious minister cannot go from home without wondering how his flock are faring during his absence. Calvin also shared this anxiety, and was made happy by hearing good accounts of all. "I congratulate myself," he wrote to the deacon who was doing duty for him during his attendance at an assembly at Worms, "and rejoice for the church's sake rather than on your account, that all attend so regularly and hear sermon reverently; for it was my chief desire and prayer, when I was about to leave, that none of our brethren whom Christ ruled by my ministry might fall off from attendance on account of my absence, that nothing of that order might be put in peril wherewith the entireness of the flock of Christ is kept together in a body." [2]

[1] Bonnet, Letter 58.

[2] *Ibid.*, Letter 57.

How he "fenced the tables,"—to employ a phrase once familiar in Scotland—in other words, how he guarded the Holy Supper from unworthy persons, is described in a delightful communication to Farel: "When the day of the Sacrament of the Supper draws nigh, I give notice from the pulpit that those who are desirous to communicate must first of all let me know, at the same time I add for what purpose, that it is in order that those who are as yet uninstructed and inexperienced in religion may be better trained; besides, that those who need special admonition may hear it; and lastly, that if there are any persons who may be suffering under trouble of mind, they may receive consolation. And to say nothing about the church, how shall the minister himself, to whom the dispensation of this grace is committed, on condition that he may not cast it before dogs and swine, that he must not pour it out to the worthy and unworthy without distinction, discharge this onerous duty, unless he proceeds upon some fixed and certain method for separating the worthy from the unworthy communicants."[1]

Calvin, we know, was a rigid disciplinarian. To him a church without discipline was no church at

[1] Bonnet, Letter 46.

all. On settling the second time in Geneva as a pastor, he immediately set about the establishment of a code of morals. Writing to Farel he says, " Immediately after I had offered my services to the Senate, I declared that a church could not hold together unless a settled government should be agreed on, such as is prescribed to us in the Word of God, and such as was in use in the ancient church. Then I touched gently on certain points from whence they might understand what my wish was. But because the whole question of discipline was too large to be discussed in that form, I requested that they would appoint certain of their number, who might confer with us on the subject." [1]

The Genevan code of discipline was severe, and had been severe long before Calvin's day, and from the state of public and private morals needed to be severe. And thus it came about that many things were forbidden, among them dancing, masquerading, games of chance, swearing, slander, and the singing of idle songs. Church attendance, at certain times, was compulsory, and the people required to be in their houses by nine at night. The registers of 1546 record the case of Amy Perrin, the Captain-

[1] Bonnet, Letter 76.

General of the city, Corna the Syndic, and others—all great friends of Calvin's at the beginning of his ministry—who were guilty of dancing in a private house, and it is minuted: "It is ordained that they all be imprisoned." From this case we see that if the laws were harsh, this was in their favour that they were impartially administered. Calvin was justly proud of the fact that there was not one law for the rich and another for the poor. A certain substantial family called Favres—connected by marriage with Amy Perrin—became involved in scandal. "I added," writes Calvin to Farel, "that a new city must be built for them, in which they might live apart, unless they were willing to be restrained by us here under the yoke of Christ; that so long as they were in Geneva they would strive in vain to cast off obedience to the laws; for were there as many diadems in the house of the Favres as frenzied heads, that that would be no barrier to the Lord being superior. Two things are already matter of public talk, that there is no hope of impunity since even the first people of the city are not spared, and that I show no more favour to friends than to those opposed to me."[1]

Calvin even deemed it necessary to support

[1] Bonnet, Letter 163.

the regulations regarding the clothing of the people. "The state of our young people," he tells Farel, "especially is very corrupt. Of late, they were sorely enraged under cover of a small matter. It was because they were not allowed to wear slashed breeches, which has been prohibited in the town for these twelve years. Not that we would make overmuch of this, but because we see that by the loop-holes of the breeches they wish to bring in all manner of disorders. We have protested, however, in the meantime, that the slashing of their breeches was but a mere piece of foppery which was not worth speaking about, but that we had quite another end in view, which was to curb and repress their follies."[1]

Not only were the morals of the Genevans bad, calling forth as we see the most severe measures for their suppression, but outbreaks of the most inhuman barbarity were not unknown. Calvin describes one of them: "A conspiracy of men and women has lately been discovered who, for the space of three years, had spread the plague through the city, by what mischievous device I know not. After fifteen women have been burned; some men have even been punished

[1] Bonnet, Letter 202.

more severely; some have committed suicide in prison, and while twenty-five are still kept prisoners, the conspirators do not cease notwithstanding to smear the door-locks of the dwelling-houses with their poisonous ointment. You see in the midst of what perils we are tossed about. The Lord hath hitherto preserved our dwelling, though it has more than once been attempted. It is well that we know ourselves to be under His care."[1]

Some of Calvin's colleagues in Geneva outstripped him in their puritanical zeal. We read of a morality play—*The Acts of the Apostles*—being acted in the city, which enjoyed the patronage of some of the ministers. But one zealot, Michael Cop, denounced it from the pulpit of St. Peter's, and characterised the actresses engaged in it as *shameless creatures.* This was too much for his hearers, who suddenly became excited to the verge of riotousness. "A concourse of people straightway made towards me," says Calvin, "with loud shouts, threats, and what not. And had I not by a strong effort restrained the fury of some of them, they would have come to blows."[2] Michael was near being killed by the excited populace. Calvin evidently regarded the

[1] Bonnet, Letter 129. [2] *Ibid.*, Letter 167.

whole thing as much ado about nothing, and set himself "to restore our furious friend to sanity."

If life in Geneva was hard for those who indulged in libertine inclinations, and church and civic authority alike applied the thumbscrew of prohibition with relentless severity, the administrators of the law were not less hard upon themselves than they were on the people over whom they ruled with a rod of iron. By the time that John Knox was exercising his ministry in Geneva, he describes an ordinance that was imposed on the English congregation over which he was for a time pastor. "To the intent that the ministrie of Gode's Woorde may be had in reverence, and not brought to contempt through the evill conversation of suche as are called therunto, and also that fautes and vices may not by long sufferance growe at length to extreme inconveniences, it is ordeyned that every Thursday the ministers and elders, in their Assembly or Consistorie, diligentlie examine all such fautes and suspicions as may be espied, not onlie amongest others but chieflie amongest theymselves, lest they seme to be culpable of that which our Saviour Christ reproved in the Pharisies, who could espie a mote in an other man's eye, and coulde not see a beame in their owne."

CHAPTER V

THE REFORMER

WE may roughly divide Calvin's career into three stages. In the first he laboured at a re-statement of the ancient Christian doctrine. In the second he set himself to reconstruct the social fabric of his city, where the truth might find something like a worthy expression. And in the latest stage we find him looking abroad upon the world and proclaiming in its hearing the duty of Christian union and confederation.

His work was beset with difficulties. By his time the wave of enthusiasm that bore Luther forward to his goal had died down. A period of reaction had set in. A strong prejudice against the Reformation had been aroused by the German peasant revolt. Anabaptism with its alluring sophistries was sweeping multitudes into its net. The Reformed party was a kingdom divided within itself, Lutheran was warring with Zwinglian, and Calvinist with both. Signs of revival were appearing within the old Catholic communion. The wise men among the priesthood were setting their house in order, and the church was recovering from the assault inflicted on her by Luther. With all these counter-influences to face, Calvin had not an easy time of it. His was not a bed of roses. He required to have great faith, not a little dexterity, and unbounded courage. When he spoke, no one, not even the occupier of a throne, should be allowed to silence him. When he gave his decision, not the strongest organised conspiracy must be allowed to intimidate him.

Once the Queen of Navarre attempted to gag him, but he wrote a letter telling her that "a dog barks and stands at bay if he sees any one assault his master. I should be indeed remiss if, seeing the truth of God thus attacked, I should remain dumb, without giving one note of warning."[1] That Calvin believed with Cromwell's men in trusting in God and keeping the powder dry is plain from what he wrote to Farel. At the time it looked as if Satan might conquer after all and God be defeated. "If, however," he said, "from one monstrous head a hundred were to spring, and if for every one head even a thousand were to threaten us, we know for certain, that while we wage war under the banner of our Christ, and fight with the weapons of His warfare, we shall be unconquerable. At the

[1] Bonnet, Letter 130.

same time, however, we must keep in mind that we ought to omit nothing by which we may oppose and frustrate the crafty devices of our enemy."[1]

Calvin was a prince of controversialists, and in this capacity he is seen to best advantage in his famous letter to Sadolet. James Sadolet was Bishop of Carpentras, a region situated to the north-east of Avignon. In recognition of his personal character, no less than of his statecraft and eloquence, he had been presented with a cardinal's hat. He was a deep man, who was always working in the interests of his church. A cleverer plotter than any of his age, his most brilliant sally was when he attempted to recapture Geneva during Calvin's enforced absence from it. To accomplish his ambitious scheme he addressed a letter to the Senate and people of Geneva, in which he employed every argument that a subtle and designing priest could command in order to recall them to allegiance to Rome. Without mentioning Calvin's name, he attacked the gospel preached by him to the Genevans as a farrago of impious dogmas. He shamelessly imputed feelings of spitefulness to the Reformers: and declared that they turned

[1] Bonnet, Letter 82.

against the church through mortification at not having secured for themselves preferment in it. In short, he omitted nothing that craft and unscrupulousness could devise for breaking down the loyalty of the Genevans to their reformed faith.

The Genevans now found themselves in a rather awkward situation. They had put away from them the only man who could give the cardinal's letter an adequate reply. Could they have the face to call him now to their aid? Luckily for them Calvin did not wait to be asked. A copy of Sadolet's letter had come into his hands at Strassburg. He read it with amazed and indignant feelings; he sat down to reply to it. In six days' time he produced a reply which was nothing short of a monument of genius. The pamphlet bore its message over Europe quicker than fire. Luther read it and was thrilled. "Here," said he, "is a writing which has hands and feet. I rejoice that God raises up such men. They will continue what I have begun against Antichrist, and by the help of God they will finish it."

Calvin, in his letter of reply to Sadolet, smote the enemy hip and thigh. He spared him nothing; let nothing pass. Repelling the hateful and slanderous charge of wounded vanity, he told Sadolet: "I am unwilling to speak of myself, but since you do not permit me to be altogether silent, I will say what I can consistent with modesty. Had I wished to consult my own interest, I would never have left your party. I will not, indeed, boast that there the road to preferment had been easy to me. I never desired it, and I never could bring my mind to catch at it: although I certainly know not a few of my own age who have crept up to some eminence—among them some whom I might have equalled, and others outstripped. This only I will be contented to say, it would not have been difficult for me to reach the summit of my wishes, viz., the enjoyment of literary ease with something of a free and honourable station. Therefore, I have no fear that any one not possessed of shameless effrontery will object to me, that out of the kingdom of the Pope I sought for any personal advantage which was not there ready to my hand." The Genevan gospel had been called a farrago of impious dogmas. Calvin gives a truer account of it. "We bid a man begin by examining himself. Thus confounded, he is humbled before God. Then we show that the only haven of safety is in the mercy of God.

Man is reconciled in Christ to God the Father by no merit of his own, by no value of good works, but by gratuitous mercy. What have you here, Sadolet, to bite or carp at?" Calvin then tells him that he would be a better theologian if he had more experience of a living and struggling conscience. The wound that rankled sorest in Calvin's flesh, however, was the imputation cast on his honour and honesty. At the end of the letter he again deals with it. He hurls back the charge into his enemy's vital parts. "What! Would not the shortest road to riches and honours have been to have transacted with you at the very first on the terms which were offered? How much would your pontiff then have paid to many for their silence? How much would he pay for it even at the present day? If they are actuated in the least degree by avarice, why do they cut off all hope of improving their fortune, and prefer to be thus perpetually wretched rather than enrich themselves without difficulty and in a twinkling? But ambition, forsooth, withholds them! What ground you had for this other insinuation I see not, since those who first engaged in this cause could expect nothing else than to be spurned by the whole world, and those who afterwards adhered to it exposed themselves knowingly and willingly to endless insults and revilings from every quarter. But where is this fraud and inward malice? No suspicion of such things cleaves to us. Talk of them rather in your sacred Consistory where they are in operation every day."

In Calvin's letters we have the different Imperial Diets sketched, and the gatherings are brought vividly before our eye. In response to the invitation of the Emperor Charles V., the Protestant princes of Germany met in conference with distinguished representatives of the Catholic and Protestant churches with a view to arriving at a better understanding of the situation of affairs. The conferences generally ended in smoke, at least so far as the work of reconciliation was concerned, but the emperor's aim was a noble one, and one worthy of a brave attempt at realisation.

The first of the gatherings was convened at Frankfort in 1539. Thither repaired Calvin and a little company of keen-minded theologians from Strassburg. Calvin was more bent on making Melanchthon's acquaintance than attending the Diet. The emperor was represented on the occasion by an archbishop. Luther's friend, the Elector of Saxony, was there with a retinue of 400 horsemen. Calvin, speaking in one of his letters of the grandees whom he saw, tells us of one whom he did not see. "There were few, however, who did not feel indignant that the Duke of Wurtemberg preferred rather to enjoy his field sports in hunting, and I know not what other sportive recreations, than to be present at the conference, in which both his native country and perhaps his life are concerned, when he was only two days' journey distant." [1]

Hagenau (in June 1540), and Worms (in October of the same year), were the scenes of the next conventions, both, however, proving abortive.

More serious business was attempted at Ratisbon in April 1541. Calvin describes the gathering of notables in his letter to Farel. "The embassies from foreign nations," he tells him, "are many and magnificent. The Cardinal Contarini" (a prelate of great moderation and enlightenment) "is legate from the Pope, who has distributed so many crosses for us at his first entrance, that for two days afterwards his arm, I think, must have felt the fatigue of it. Contarini is desirous of bringing us under the yoke of subjection without bloodshed. On that

[1] Bonnet, Letter 32.

account he tries all methods of settling the business on the ground of expediency, without having recourse to arms. The Venetians have an ambassador here—a magnificent personage. The King of England, besides the ordinary embassy to the Diet, has sent the Bishop of Winchester, with a numerous suite, who is a man over-sharp in malice. I pass by the Portuguese and others. From the French king also there is one Du Veil, a busy blockhead."[1]

At this Diet considerable agreement was evinced by the different parties on the vexed questions that separated them. "The debate was more keen upon the doctrine of justification. At length a formula was drawn up, which, on receiving certain corrections, was accepted on both sides. You will be astonished, I am sure, that our opponents have yielded so much, when you read the extracted copy, as it stood when the last correction was made upon it, which you will find enclosed in the letter. Our friends have thus retained also the substance of the true doctrine, so that nothing can be comprehended within it which is not to be found in our writings. You will desire, I know, a more distinct explication and statement of the doctrine, and, in that

[1] Bonnet, Letter 63.

respect, you shall find me in complete agreement with yourself. However, if you consider with what kind of men we have to agree upon this doctrine, you will acknowledge that much has been accomplished."[1] Transubstantiation, however, proved, as usual, "the impassable rock which barred the way to farther progress." He adds: "I had also to explain in Latin what were my sentiments," on the subject of the real presence in the sacrament. "Although I had not understood any one of the others, deliberately, without fear of offence, I condemned that peculiar local presence; the act of adoration I declared to be altogether insufferable. Believe me, in matters of this kind, boldness is absolutely necessary for strengthening and confirming others."[2]

Nothing was accomplished at these conferences compared to what the promoters of them hoped for. Any *via media* was seen to be an idle dream. The earnest men on both sides were not worldly politicians, but religious dogmatists. The matters in debate were to them questions of life and death. Compromise, therefore, in the circumstances was not possible, nor even desirable.

Those troublers in Israel known as Libertines

[1] Bonnet, Letter 67.

[2] *Ibid.*, Letter 67.

are a frequent subject of talk in Calvin's letters between 1546 and 1553. They are a mournful example of the depths of moral turpitude into which religious fanaticism will drive people. Under the plea of *the right of private judgment* they claimed liberty to determine what acts were and what were not immoral. Some, though not all of them, maintained that on principle they had the right if they chose to lead a life of licentiousness. By the communion of saints they understood the common possession of goods, houses, bodies, and wives. They had the audacity to carry their principles into practice. They practised adultery and indulged in sexual promiscuity, while at the same time they held up an unabashed countenance in the church, and claimed the right to sit at the Lord's table.

Here, then, the Purifier of Genevan morals found himself confronted with a more hideous enemy than the papacy even. But he stood his ground unmoved. With unflinching nerve he wielded his sword of resistance. Through a deluge of personal abuse and many threats of murder, he pursued his course of reform and social regeneration.

He had never shouted the watchword, *the right of private judgment.* It was not according to

Scripture, and no church could be worked on such a principle. If there were doubtful questions touching faith or morals, these were to be resolved, according to Calvin, not by individuals, but by a council of true bishops—*verorum episcoporum synodus* (*Inst.* IV. 9). For nine long years Libertinism proved a scandal in Geneva, and Calvin's efforts to stamp it out went on till they were victorious, although at a terrible cost to his health and strength. During this miserable time the dispensation of the Lord's Supper was often made a scene of disturbance, through the necessity that there was for the Libertines being debarred from partaking of the holy ordinance. There were times during this period when Calvin grew so sick of the strife that he tells us he could willingly have fled from it all. "We are to celebrate the supper on the Lord's day," he writes to that unfailing friend, Farel. "Would that it could be celebrated without me, even on condition that I should creep to you on my hands." [1] Towards the close of the Libertine conflicts, one Berthelier, who had been interdicted from the Lord's Supper on account of his immoral life, appealed from the decision of the Consistory to that of the magistrates or Council of State.

[1] Bonnet, Letter 163.

Berthelier was successful in his suit, the ecclesiastical sentence was annulled, and he was declared entitled to go forward to the sacrament. During Calvin's absence an opportunity was afforded him of receiving the Supper. "As soon as I got notice of it," Calvin tells Viret, "I used all my endeavours to get the Syndics to call a meeting of the Senate. I endeavoured, partly by vehemence and partly by moderation, to reduce them to a sound mind. I even took an oath that I had resolved rather to meet death than profane so shamefully the holy Supper of the Lord; for that nothing was more intolerable than that that individual, mocking and insulting the Church of God by his contumacy, should, by raising the standard, so to speak, incite the worst characters, and those like himself, to indulge in the same effrontery. The reply was that the Senate had nothing to change in its former decision. From which you perceive that by this law my ministry is abandoned if I suffer the authority of the Consistory to be trampled upon, and extend the Supper of Christ to open scoffers, who boast that pastors are nothing to them. In truth, I should rather die a hundred times than subject Christ to such foul mockery."[1]

[1] Bonnet, Letter 323.

A memorable scene was enacted in the Cathedral of St. Peter's at this time in connection with the celebration of the Lord's Supper. Berthelier and other Libertines were present in the church prepared when the time came to defy the authority of the ministers. It was indeed a critical moment for the future of the Reformed religion. The sermon had been preached, the prayers had been offered, and Calvin descended from the pulpit to take his place beside the elements at the communion table. The bread and wine were duly consecrated by him, and he was now ready to distribute them to the communicants. Then on a sudden a rush was begun by the troublers in Israel in the direction of the communion table. It seemed as if they aimed at snatching up the bread and the cup in their hand. Calvin flung his arms around the sacramental vessels as if to protect them from sacrilege, while his voice rang through the building: "These hands you may crush, these arms you may lop off, my life you may take, my blood is yours, you may shed it; but you shall never force me to give holy things to the profane, and dishonour the table of my God." After this, says Beza, Calvin's first biographer, "the sacred ordinance was celebrated with a profound silence, and under a solemn awe in all present, as if the Deity Himself had been visible among them."

The union of Christians and Christian churches was one of the objects for which Calvin exerted himself with almost as much vigour as he did for sound doctrine and well-regulated human lives. Few things astonished him more than the want of agreement among the Reformed party. He regarded schism as a serious sin. What have we profited, he asks Bullinger, by shaking off the tyranny of the Pope if we are to be dominated by miserable schismatics? A merchant, he tells Melanchthon, showed him recently a bitter partisan pamphlet written by one of their professors, "of which I felt greatly ashamed. For what good purpose could it serve to assault the Zwinglians every third line, and to attack Zwingli himself in such an unmannerly style? and not even to spare Oecolampadius, that holy servant of God, whom I wish that he resembled, even in being half as good, in which case he would certainly stand far higher in my esteem than he does. O God of grace, what pleasant sport and pastime do we afford to the Papists, as if we had hired ourselves to do their work!" [1]

The unity of the Papacy—although attained

[1] Bonnet, Letter 123.

by methods that Protestants could not look at—gave the Roman Church a great advantage in the prosecution of her work. What enterprises of great pith and moment were possible to an organisation that all the world over was one and undivided. Calvin saw this and longed for unity among the Protestant churches. For this he pleaded in the pulpit to great and influential congregations, for this he prepared conciliatory formulas of the faith, for this he attended far-distant synods and diets. And although at the time it evoked no sympathetic response, that was a noble letter which he addressed from the church at Geneva to the synod at Berne: "Since we both preach the same Christ, both profess the same gospel, are both members of the same church and have both the same ministry, there ought not to be that diversity of authority among us to which we have been subject, either to break up the unity of our faith, or to hinder from flourishing amongst us so many rights of holy fellowship consecrated to the service of Christ. That proximity of residence also, which is so influential among the children of this world, into drawing them into close friendship, ought not at least to be less powerful among us." [1]

[1] Bonnet, Letter 237.

The same year (1549) Farel and he met Bullinger in Zurich, and together drew up the famous *Consensus,* which sought so to present the doctrine of the Sacrament as to unite the churches of the Reformation, and which was well received in France, England, and even in parts of Germany. Nor was Calvin's dream of a united Protestant church a local and limited one. He desired to see the churches of Germany, France, Switzerland, England, and Scotland united. "The members of the Church," he writes to Cranmer, "being severed, the body lies bleeding. So much does this concern me that could I be of any service, I would not grudge to cross even ten seas if need were on account of it."[1]

Calvin manifested a keen interest in the progress of Reformation in England and Scotland, and we have abundant illustration of this in his letters. How closely he followed the work in Scotland, and how intimate he was with John Knox will be shown in our last chapter. Here let us note how, when dark clouds rested over the Reformed churches of the continent, when Libertinism was rampant in Geneva, when the voice of Luther that shook the papacy to its

[1] Bonnet, Letter 293.

F

foundations was now still in death, and a tide of reaction had set in in the Fatherland, at that time Calvin turned with hopeful gaze to England, to its gracious primate, and to its religiously-minded young King Edward. He entered into communication with Edward and with the Lord Protector Somerset, by whom Calvin's advice is solicited. To Somerset he dedicated one of his commentaries; and on Calvin's recommendation Somerset found in England a home for Bucer, Peter Martyr, and other refugees. Somerset fell the victim of Warwick's ambition, and died on the scaffold in 1552. In one of his letters—which contains no fewer than 6000 words—he advises Somerset as to the disposal of rebels. "From what I am given to understand, monseigneur, there are two kinds of rebels who have risen up against the king and the estates of the kingdom. The one a fantastical sort of person who, under colour of the gospel, would put all into confusion. The others are persons who persist in the superstitions of the Roman Antichrist." And then follows advice which all our readers will disapprove: "Both alike deserve to be repressed by the sword which is committed to you, since they not only attack the king, but strive with God, who has placed him upon a royal throne, and has committed to you the protection as well of his person as of his majesty."[1]

After Somerset had been temporarily liberated from the Tower, Calvin sent him another voluminous epistle, in the course of which he speaks to him as a duke has seldom been spoken to by a humble servant of Christ. In this letter Calvin's advice will compare favourably with that given in the previous one. How well he pleads with his Grace to forgive his enemies and return good for evil: "It is not I alone who rejoice at the good issue which God has given to your affliction, but all true believers, who desire the advancement of the kingdom of our Lord Jesus Christ, forasmuch as they know the solicitude with which you have laboured for the re-establishing of the gospel in all its purity in England, and that every kind of superstition might be abolished I know how you may be tempted to render the like to those whom you reckon to have meditated greater mischief against you than what has come to pass. But you know the admonition which Saint Paul has given us on that head, that is, that we have not to fight against flesh and blood, but against the hidden wiles of our spiritual enemy. Therefore, monseigneur, forgetting and pardon-

[1] Bonnet, Letter 229.

ing the faults of those whom you may conceive to have been your enemies, apply your whole mind to repel his malice who thus engaged them to their own destruction in setting themselves to seek your ruin. This magnanimity will not only be pleasing to God, but it will make you the more loved among men; and I do not doubt that you have such regard to that as you ought." [1]

Calvin wrote several letters to King Edward. In one he commended to him the example of King Josiah. In another he gave him advice as to the providing of pastors " that the poor flocks may not be destitute of pastors." In another he wrote in behalf of a countryman of his own, who was detained a prisoner in Paris, asking him to use his influence with the King of France. But the finest of his communications to the young King was an exhortation couched in terms of faithful affection. " It is a great thing, sire, to be a king, and especially of such a country: and yet I doubt not that you regard it as above all comparison greater to be a Christian. It is indeed an inestimable privilege that God has granted to you, sire, that you should be a Christian king, and that you should serve Him as His lieutenant to uphold the kingdom of Jesus Christ in England."

[1] Bonnet, Letter 257.

CHAPTER VI

THE FRIEND

ALTHOUGH Calvin made many mortal enemies, he appears to have had some genius for friendship too. That he made many enemies, and could not avoid making them, goes without saying. Like Dante, who thought nothing of putting his own friends among the damned in *Inferno*, when the requirements of justice demanded it, so Calvin could be inexorably unmerciful whenever he supposed that the honour of God was involved. One who came under the lash of his tongue in a public controversy was wont afterwards to declare that he knew Calvin and Beza well, but that he would rather be in hell with Beza than in heaven with Calvin. A report of Calvin's death made multitudes delirious with joy. When a false rumour of this kind got abroad in 1551, a day of thanksgiving was proclaimed in his native place, and a solemn procession of the canons of the cathedral took place. Even Grotius, philosopher as he was, must have had a mortal dislike to Calvin, if he really did say what is placed to his credit, that the spirit of Antichrist had been seen, not on the banks of the Tiber only, but on those of lake Leman.

And yet truer and more disinterested friends never existed than William Farel, Peter Viret, and John Calvin. In 1549, Calvin dedicated his commentary on the *Epistle to Titus* to these two staunch men, and said in the Preface: " I do not think that there have been friends who have lived together in such fast friendship as we have done during our ministry. I have been a fellow-pastor here with both of you. So far from there having been any appearance of envy between you and me, I always regarded us as one. As for you, Master William, the church of Neuchatel, which you have delivered from the tyranny of the Papacy and won over to Christ, called you to be its pastor; and as for you, Master Peter, you stand in a similar relation to the church at Lausanne. Each of us, however, guards so well the place committed to us, that by our united efforts the children of God assemble within the fold of Jesus Christ, and are even united in one company."

Calvin's friendship was of the robust type that could survive through theological differences and disagreements. Thus to Bullinger, pastor at Zurich, who did not see eye to eye with him on the doctrine of Election, and was not afraid to tell him so, he wrote: "Although you disappointed my expectations, I nevertheless gladly offer you our friendship." [1]

Naturally enough, the warmest corner of his heart was reserved for those who were in more entire accord with him. His warmth for Viret rose to a high temperature. "Would that I also could fly thither" (to Lausanne), he wrote to him, "that I might alleviate your sorrow, or at least bear a part of it. But so long a ride would cause me pain. I rather advise, should matters happen otherwise than as we wish, that you come hither for a few days. Adieu, most sound-hearted brother, along with your wife and family. The Lord comfort and strengthen you all." [2] The date of this letter is February 22, 1546. In the same year—Viret having lost his wife meantime—about the beginning of March, Calvin renewed his warm invitation in these cordial terms: "Come on this condition, that you disengage your mind not only from grief, but also from every annoyance. Do not fear that I will impose any burden upon you, for through my means you will be allowed to take whatever rest is agreeable to you. If any one

[1] Bonnet, Letter 289. [2] *Ibid.*, Letter 156.

prove troublesome to you I will interpose. The brethren also make the same promise to you as I do. I will also be surety that the citizens do not interfere with your wishes. I know not what I ought to imprecate on the wretches who had spread a report of your death. Never did a letter from you arrive more opportunely. Although your death was announced, yet, as mention was made of poison, Textor was already in the midst of preparations for the journey, that he might speed to Orbe on fleet horses. A great part of the brethren were present, all overwhelmed with deep affliction. Shortly afterward your letter made its appearance, and such exultation instantly broke forth, that we were hardly masters of our senses. It was fortunate that we did not pass a night of sorrow, else I should not have borne it without danger. But why do I detain you, and not rather incite you to hasten hither as quickly as possible?"[1]

A week later, Viret not having come, Calvin with playful importunity writes: "Since I can draw you out by no other inducement, I make the announcement that you shall have no letter from me until you come!"[2] Keenly intellectual persons like Calvin are so frequently cold at the

[1] Bonnet, Letter 157. [2] *Ibid.*, Letter 158.

heart, wrapped up in themselves and indifferent to the kindly domesticalities of life, we are all the more drawn to this much misunderstood pastor at Geneva, who is so interested in the comfort of his lonely and now widowed friend that he frets and worries over it.

One of his famous friends at Geneva was Robert Stephens, the celebrated printer. He had been obliged to remove his presses to Geneva, France having become too warm for a man of his Reformation sympathies. The Sorbonne made it impossible for him to remain in Paris. He had incurred the odium of the Papacy by his beautiful edition of the Bible. He settled in Geneva, therefore, with his son Henry, at the close of the year 1550. He was made a burgess in 1556, and lived in close friendship with Calvin and Beza until his death in 1559. "Robert Stephens," he tells Farel, "is now entirely ours, and we shall soon hear what storms his departure has raised in Paris. The retiring philosophers will doubtless be quite insane." [1]

There was surely a streak of amiableness in Calvin, after all, that has been strangely overlooked. By repute a man of choleric temper, who easily yielded to anger, a good deal of the

[1] Bonnet, Letter 268.

treatment which he received in the world provoked and irritated his temper. No one knew his faults better than himself, or mourned more bitterly over them. "Of all the struggles which I have had against my failings," he once confessed, "and these struggles have been many and severe, the greatest has been that against my impatience. My efforts have not been wholly vain; but still I have not yet been able entirely to tame this wild animal." Yet numberless were his acts of kindness. Here are two. A woman who had publicly reviled him was ordered to prison by the Town Council. Calvin went to the authorities and interceded in her behalf. He succeeded in obtaining a pardon for her on the ground that the offence was not against God or the civil law, but only one personal to himself. More remarkable was the fine Christian spirit shown to Amy Perrin, who, from a friend, as we have seen, became one of Calvin's most malignant foes. Perrin had lost his place in the Senate for his misdemeanours. Calvin felt for the man, and set himself to do him a good turn. By his influence, therefore, he obtained a reversal of the sentence, and Perrin, to his surprise, found himself, by Calvin's intercession, restored to the membership of the Senate.

We are now to behold Calvin's genius for friendship blossom out in quite a romantic direction. He becomes a matchmaker! Turning aside from the more serious occupations of his life, he seeks to find a partner for the widower Viret. Viret had lost his wife in March 1546. The union had been a happy one. Recalling his grief some time afterward, he said, "I was so completely dispirited and prostrated by that arrow of affliction that the whole world appeared to me to be nothing but a burden. There was nothing pleasant, nothing that could mitigate my grief of mind."

Elizabeth Turtaz, Viret's wife, was barely four months dead when Calvin opened his matchmaking campaign. The haste seems nowadays grossly indecent. But "the whole business of marrying and giving in marriage was then carried out in a fashion that is apt to revolt the better feeling of the present day. In the case of certain of the finest spirits of the sixteenth century, we experience a shock at what seems the brutality of their relations to their wives. Sir Thomas More, the most delicate nature of his time, married his second wife within a month of the death of his first. From the histories of the leading Reformers we learn that the choice of a partner in life was as often as not entrusted to a judicious circle of friends, who did at once the part of the lawyer and the lover in bringing about the desired arrangement."[1]

These words of Professor P. Hume Brown make Calvin's eagerness as a matchmaker, and the apparently indecent haste with which he enlisted his services in behalf of his friend's matrimonial interests, somewhat more intelligible than they would otherwise be. It was in July then that he wrote to M. de Falais at Strassburg: "You know that our brother Viret is about to marry. I am in as great anxiety about it as himself. We have plenty of wives here, both at Lausanne and at Orbe; but yet there has not hitherto appeared a single one with whom I should feel at all satisfied. While we have this matter in hand, I would beseech you earnestly, if you have remarked any one in your quarter who appears to you likely to suit him, that you would please let me know of it. I have not thought fit to apply to any other than yourself, seeing that every one has not the prudence which is herein required. You may reply to me, that I am at least acquainted with some one in your neighbourhood; but I shall not venture to

[1] *John Knox*, II. 201.

breathe a word before having your opinion, which you can tell me in one word, for I shall hold your silence for a *non placet.* I have not felt the least difficulty in addressing you privately in regard to this, although the subject may be rather delicate, for the necessity of the case would excuse me, were I even somewhat importunate, because there was no one else in whom it appeared safe to confide; and I am well aware that, for your part, knowing of how much consequence the marriage of such a man is for the Church of God, you would not spare yourself any pains therein. Indeed, I would not hinder your acting directly for him, supposing that a suitable party can be found there; but in regard to asking advice, I have taken for granted that you will allow me that liberty." [1]

A week later Calvin has his eye on a wife for the widower, and he writes to him urging her charms: "Think of what you are going to do, and then write to me again what resolution you have come to. The more we inquire, the more numerous and the better are the testimonies with which the young lady is honoured. Accordingly, I am now seeking to discover the mind of her father. As soon as we have reached any

[1] Bonnet, Letter 168.

certainty I will let you know. Meanwhile, do you make yourself ready. This match does not please Perrin, because he wishes to force upon you the daughter of Rameau. That makes me the more solicitous about pre-occupying the ground in good time, lest we be obstructed by having to make excuses. To-day, as far as I gather, he will enter upon the subject with me, for we are both invited by Corna to supper. I will gain time by a civil excuse. It would tend to promote the matter if I, with your permission, should ask her. I have seen her twice: she is very modest, with an exceedingly becoming countenance and person. Of her manners, all speak so highly that John Parvi lately told me he had been captivated by her. Adieu; may the Lord govern you by His counsel, and bless us in an undertaking of such moment." [1]

In this interesting glimpse into matrimonial matters in the sixteenth century, we see the two friends of the widower playing their own little game. But he, sensible man, refuses to dance to either tune. We shall find him taking his own course, neither Calvin's fair *protégée*, nor the daughter of Rameau finding favour in his eyes! But let us finish the correspondence. Two days

[1] Bonnet, Letter 169.

after the letter just quoted, Calvin again writes to his friend, giving an account of an extraordinary scene that took place at the supper-party referred to between himself and Perrin. How strange to hear John Calvin, author of the *Institutes*, whom Bossuet called ***un génie triste,*** offering to put the question to the young lady in his friend's behalf! "Three days ago, towards the conclusion of supper, mention was made of your marriage, which I had foretold you would be the case. But Dominic Arlot, whose assistance I had employed, presently interrupted the conversation; for he said that the matter was completed. On hearing this our friend instantly sprung up from the table, and in his usual way gave reins to his indignation; for says he, his whole body shaking, 'Will he, then, marry that girl of low connections? Could there not be found for him in the city one of better family? Whoever have been the originators or abettors of this business, I regard them as vile and infamous.' I, in reply, say: 'I could not be the originator of it, inasmuch as the young lady was unknown to me. I acknowledge that I was a promoter of it, and indeed the principal one; but that the matter is finally settled, as Dominic has asserted, is not true beyond this, that I have gone so far in it that to draw back would be dishonourable. In that there is nothing for me to be ashamed of.' His fury was thus turned into laughter.

"Suppose you consent to my asking the young lady in your name, the condition being added that before the betrothal takes place, you are to meet her, that we may give some certain promise. Of the lady I hear nothing that is not highly pleasing. There are some things about the daughter of Rameau which I fear; nevertheless, as it is your own affair, you will be free to choose. I will never, however, allow that there is any man on earth who has greater concern about his own matters than I have about the present." [1]

In November, 1546, Viret was married to Elizabeth Laharpe, the daughter of a French refugee of Lausanne. Calvin attended the wedding and gave the nuptial benediction. But why was the lady of Calvin's choice not the bride? That is fully explained by Calvin. "After reading your letter," he tells Viret, "I waited on the father and daughter, that I might be absolutely certain of success. As soon, however, as reference was made to a change of

[1] Bonnet, Letter 170.

residence, the father took exception to it. I pointed out how absurd it would be to leave our churches to follow whither our wives called us. I added that Lausanne was not so far distant from this as to prevent his daughter from being with him as often as might be necessary." But the father was firm: he was not willing to allow his daughter to leave the city. Calvin quaintly adds: "I felt greatly indignant at being so deluded by the folly of those in whom I trusted. I restrained myself, however, and dissembled my anger. We may accordingly turn to some other quarter. Christopher spoke to me of a certain widow, who, he asserts, pleases him admirably."[1]

Calvin did not press the widow's suit, but allowed his friend to choose for himself, or, as he puts it, he "let the stream find its own channel"; and yet talking of the widow afterwards to his friend De Falais he confesses that she was "as well endowed as I could have wished for myself if God had so far afflicted me as to have deprived me of my helpmate, and that there was a necessity for me marrying again."[2]

Our extracts from Calvin's letters bearing upon his character as a friend would be incomplete without a sample of his frankness and

[1] Bonnet, Letter 172. [2] *Ibid.*, Letter 178.

candour, a sterling quality of all sincere friendship. He is writing to Farel, a man twenty years his senior, and he addresses to him a friendly remonstrance on the undue length of his sermons. Farel was an orator, and had an extemporaneous speaker's fatal fluency, and Calvin warns him against tediousness. Notice the fine thought about keeping our lengthy prayers for private use instead of parading them before others in public. "I understand the prolixity of your discourses has furnished ground of complaint to many. I beg and beseech of you to strive to restrain yourself. Since the Lord commands us to ascend the pulpit not for our own edification, but for that of the people, you should so regulate the manner of your teaching that the Word may not be brought into contempt by your tediousness. It is more appropriate also for us to lengthen our prayers in private, than when we offer them in the name of the whole Church. You are mistaken if you expect from all an ardour equal to your own." [1]

[1] Bonnet, Letter 290.

CHAPTER VII

CALVIN AND SERVETUS

We come now to the mournful story of Calvin and Servetus, and what better can we say, to begin with, than what was uttered long ago by some of Calvin's own friends and fellow-citizens: "Would to God we could extinguish this burning pile with our tears!"

Seven years prior to the time when Servetus met his cruel fate (1553), Calvin and he had carried on a correspondence with one another, both under assumed names—Calvin adopting that of Charles d'Espeville and Servetus that of John Frellon. It began by the latter sending to Calvin an extract from his work, *Christianisimi Restitutio*—then in preparation—and expressing at the same time a desire to visit Geneva. On the day on which Calvin replied to him, he wrote to Farel about Servetus and his proposed visit, uttering a fearful threat: "Servetus lately wrote to me, and coupled with his letter a long volume of his delirious fancies, with the Thrasonic boast that I should see something astonishing and unheard of. He takes it upon him to come hither, if it be agreeable to me. But I am unwilling to pledge my word for his safety, for if he shall come, I shall never permit him to depart alive, provided my authority be of any avail." [1]

Without pausing in the meantime to characterise this cruel outburst on the part of Calvin, let us see in what terms he replied to the letter of Servetus. Speaking of him in the third person, this was what he said: "I do assure you that there is no lesson which is more necessary for him" (that is, Servetus) "than to learn humility, which must come to him from the spirit of God, not otherwise. But we must observe a measure here also. If God grants that favour to him and to us, that the present answer turns to his profit, I shall have whereof to rejoice. If he persists in the same style as he has now done, you will lose time in asking me to bestow labour upon him, for I have other affairs which press upon me more closely; and I would make a matter of conscience of it, not to busy myself further, having no doubt that it was a temptation of Satan to distract and withdraw me from other more useful reading." [2] This was in better form than the letter to Farel just quoted, though far from being in a conciliatory temper.

[1] Bonnet, Letter 154. [2] *Ibid.*, Letter 153.

Seven years later Calvin informs us about Servetus' ongoings in the interval, and how he has been filling up his cup of iniquity. In a letter "to his dearly beloved the pastors of the Church of Frankfort, Calvin outlines the career of Servetus, and passes condemnation on his errors: "You have doubtless heard of the name of Servetus, a Spaniard, who, twenty years ago, corrupted your Germany with a virulent publication, filled with many pernicious errors. This worthless fellow, after being driven out of Germany, and having concealed himself in France under a fictitious name, lately patched up a larger volume, partly from his former book, and partly from new figments which he had invented. This book he printed secretly at Vienne, a town in the neighbourhood of Lyons. Many copies of it had been conveyed to Frankfort for the Easter fairs. The printer's agent, however, a pious and worthy man, on being informed that it contained nothing but a farrago of errors, suppressed whatever he had of it. It would take long to relate with how many errors—yea, prodigious blasphemies against God—the book abounds. Figure to yourselves a rhapsody patched up from the impious ravings of all ages. There is no sort of impiety which this monster has not raked up as if from the infernal regions. I had rather you should pass sentence on it from reading the book itself. You will certainly find, on almost every single page, what will inspire you with horror. The author himself is held in prison by our magistrates, and he will be punished ere long, I hope; but it is your duty to see to it that this pestiferous poison does not spread farther. The messenger will inform you respecting the number and the repository of the books. The bookseller, if I mistake not, will permit them to be burnt. Should anything stand in the way, however, I trust that you will act so judiciously as to purge the world of such noxious corruptions. Besides, your way will be clear, because, if the matter be submitted to your judgment, there will be no necessity for asking the magistrate to interfere." [1]

What, it will be asked, were the errors of this "monster" of impiety? Probably what brought him to his doom was not so much his errors as the blasphemies with which they were interlarded. A well-educated Spaniard, with scientific knowledge far in advance of his age, though he was a deserter from the Catholic faith, Servetus had not fallen in with Protestantism. The Re-

[1] Bonnet, Letter 322.

formed party, he considered, had only done half their work. Having renounced Popery, they should have gone farther, and cut themselves free from errors on the subject of the Godhead. This step he himself had taken in his work, *Errors in the Doctrine of the Trinity.* The theology of Servetus was pantheistic. In the Trinity there were not three Persons, which he considered would have been equivalent to tritheism, but three dispositions or modifications of the Divine Being. It was not consistent with such a view of God to believe in the curse of sin or in the need for redemption. An Arian doctrine of the person of Christ was bad enough, and by no means to be tolerated in the sixteenth century either by Papist or by Protestant; but this was not the head and front of the "monster's" offence. The horror aroused by his teaching arose from the scurrilous blasphemies with which it was served up. How could Reformers of the faith tolerate one who described Christ as an *idol,* who spoke of the Trinity as a *Cerberus,* a *hellish monster,* who characterised the baptism of infants as a *devilish invention.* "If the Word had become flesh as a woman," said he, "then they would have called the Word itself the Son of God, and the woman herself the daughter of man. Hence the Son of God would have been of two sexes! In like manner, if the angels were to take asses' bodies, they would be asses. So too God might be an ass, and the Holy Ghost a mule! Can we be surprised if the Turks think us more ridiculous than asses and mules?" It was to be expected that Calvin's fury would know no bounds. In a letter to Sulzer at this time (1553) he thus broke out: "As Michael Servetus, twenty years ago, infected the Christian world with his virulent and pestilential opinions, I should suppose his name is not unknown to you. While you may not have read his book, yet you must have heard something of the sort of doctrines contained in it. It was he whom that faithful minister of Christ, Master Bucer of holy memory, in other respects of a mild disposition, declared from the pulpit to be worthy of having his bowels pulled out and torn to pieces. While he has not permitted any of his poison to go abroad since that time, he has lately, however, brought out a larger volume, printed secretly at Vienne, but patched up from the same errors. To be sure, as soon as the thing became known, he was cast into prison. He escaped from it some way or other, and wandered in Italy for nearly four months. He at length, in an evil hour, came to this place, when, at my instigation, one of the Syndics ordered him to be conducted to prison. For I do not disguise it, that I considered it my duty to put a check, so far as I could, upon this most obstinate and ungovernable man, that his contagion might not spread farther."[1] Calvin's part and lot in the tragedy that followed is here set forth in all undisguised plainness. If Servetus be nowadays regarded as a martyr in the cause of liberty of conscience, Calvin at the time claimed it as a duty that devolved upon him to restrain him, even by force, from injuring the souls of men.

Of the trial and execution of Servetus little need be said. He seems to have walked right into his enemies' arms, having been arrested on his way through Geneva, on what mission bound was never clear. Calvin's own servant, Nicolas de la Fontaine, became criminal prosecutor in the case, in conformity with judicial usages then in operation in Geneva, summoned him on a capital charge, and, according to the *lex talionis*, went to prison with him. Nicolas brought forty charges against him, which he attempted to evade. Calvin and others were called as witnesses. To Calvin Servetus was inclined to be

[1] Bonnet, Letter 325.

insolent. "I answered him," said the former, "as he deserved." The Senate found all the charges proven, and Nicolas was set free. "Of the man's effrontery, I will say nothing; but such was his madness that he did not hesitate to say that devils possessed divinity: yea, that many gods were individual devils, inasmuch as deity had been substantially communicated to those, equally with wood and stone. I hope that sentence of death will at least be passed upon him; but I desire that the severity of the punishment may be mitigated."[1]

Before putting Servetus to death, the Churches of Berne, Zurich, Schaffhausen, and Basel were consulted. All were of the opinion that Servetus was worthy of death. Even Melanchthon approved of the deed. "I am wholly of your opinion," he told Calvin, "and declare also that your magistrates acted quite justly in condemning the blasphemer to death." The unaltered law of the Christian countries of Europe was in favour of the punishment of the traitor, and of all forms of treason, heresy was regarded as one of the worst and the most dangerous. Burning for heresy was the law of the Inquisition, and it was this principle that triumphed when Ser-

[1] Bonnet, Letter 320 (*vid.* Letter 393).

vetus was put to death. That Calvin, in consenting to the death of Servetus, acted according to his light may quite freely be conceded. That in so consenting his action was justifiable, no one will admit. Nothing is more certain than that Calvin did wrong, unless it be that his friends and admirers have ever since repented of the wrong. The Protestants of Switzerland and France in 1903 raised a memorial, which they named a *monument expiatoire,* in honour of Servetus, whom they regarded as a victim of sixteenth-century bigotry. On the monument they wrote an inscription in praise of Calvin, *notre grand réformateur,* but condemning his error. Surely, Calvin was a great man and a Reformer to whom the world is indebted, and yet it is true that in the affair of Servetus he acted the part of the blind and bloody zealot. He was too much under the influence of Old Testament intolerance and too little under that of New Testament patience and love. The illustrious Genevan divine could have learnt a lesson from the humble parson in *Old Mortality,* the Rev. Mr. Poundtext. " By what law," says Henry Morton to Balfour of Burley, " would you justify the atrocity you would commit? " " If thou art ignorant of it," replied Burley, " thy companion is well aware of the law which gave the men of Jericho to the sword of Joshua the son of Nun." "Yes; but we," answered the divine, "live under a better dispensation, which instructeth us to return good for evil, and to pray for those who despitefully use us and persecute us."

CHAPTER VIII

CALVIN AND HIS BROTHER REFORMERS

On the interesting subject of his relations to the other Reformers, especially to Martin Luther, to John Knox, and to Philip Melanchthon, there is much for us to glean in the letters of Calvin.

I. To all outward appearance there seems little affinity between Luther and Calvin. How different the upbringing of the two men—the one, the son of a German miner, singing for his livelihood under the windows of the well-to-do burghers; the other, the son of a French procurator-fiscal, delicately reared and educated with the children of the nobility. How different, too, their temperaments—Luther, hearty, jovial, jocund, sociable, filling his goblet day by day from the Town Council's wine-cellar; Calvin, lean, austere, retiring, given to fasting and wakefulness. Their stars of destiny again how unlike—Luther had many good friends at court, and his path on the whole was smooth and pleasant; Calvin lived in a whirl of strife, antagonisms, scheming, and intrigue. Once more—Luther was a man of the people, endowed with passion, poetry, imagination, fire; whereas Calvin was cold, refined, courteous, able to speak to nobles and address crowned heads, and seldom, if ever, needing to retract or even to regret his words.

But in respect of unworldly ambition, both men were extremely like one another. The Elector John once sent a new coat to Luther. On receiving it he wrote in return that his friends were all too kind to him, and that if he got so much here, he feared there was little he could look forward to hereafter! It was the same with Calvin. Once a cardinal called on him at his house in Geneva. The prince of the church expected to find him residing in a palace like himself, surrounded by servants. What was his surprise to find the great theologian of Europe living in a humble tenement, with no one to open the door but himself!

Luther had more of humanity's failings in him than Calvin. He had bad fits of despondency and gloom like other men, and at times doubted the truth of what he was in the habit of preaching to the flock. Calvin never doubted the doctrines of the faith. The religious atmosphere in which he lived was always serene and unclouded.

It has sometimes been thought that the

German Luther, with his sunny temperament, would have suited the French taste better than Calvin; and that, on the other hand, the latter, with his shrewd and practical turn of mind, his precision and love of truth, would have found himself in a more congenial atmosphere in Germany. There is something to be said for this. The Germans have usually understood and appreciated Calvin fully as well as his own countrymen did. And Heine found it quite easy to interest the Parisians in "our great master, Martin Luther." Perhaps, however, the truth is that the men and their environment required to be in some little antagonism to each other, in order that the work which they were sent to do might be effectually done. Luther's work in the Fatherland needed enthusiasm, and Calvin could not have established his theocracy in Geneva had he been an indulgent man, who shut his eyes at the evil that was happening around him.

The two men never met, but they knew and valued each other's work. Calvin was in the habit of saying that though Luther were to call him a devil he would still honour him as an illustrious servant of God. He asks Bullinger to consider how eminent a man Luther was and the excellent endowments which he possessed. At the same time, he was not blind to Luther's faults, for in the same letter he says: "Would that he had been more observant and careful in the acknowledgment of his own vices. Flatterers have done him much mischief, since he is naturally too prone to be over-indulgent to himself. It is our part, however, so to reprove whatsoever evil qualities may beset him as that we may make some allowance for him at the same time on the score of these remarkable endowments with which he has been gifted." [1]

Calvin differed from Luther on many points, notably on the doctrine of the Lord's Supper, but he was ever impressing his colleagues with the duty of respecting and reverencing Luther. Luther to him was ever "a distinguished servant of Christ, to whom we are all of us largely indebted." That Luther appreciated him was a source of delight to him. Writing to Farel he says: "Crato, one of our engravers, lately returned from Wittemberg, brought a letter from Luther to Bucer in which there was written: 'Salute for me reverently Sturm and Calvin, whose books I have read with special delight.' Now consider seriously what I have said there about the Eucharist; think of the ingenuousness

[1] Bonnet, Letter 122.

of Luther. It will now be easy for you to see how unreasonable are those who so obstinately dissent from him." [1]

Some busybody, wishing to irritate Luther, showed him a passage in which he and his friends had been criticised by Calvin; whereupon Luther, after having examined the passage, said: "I hope that Calvin will one day think better of us; but in any event, it is well that he should even now have a proof of our good feeling towards him." This generous remark greatly pleased Calvin. "If we are not affected," he wrote, "by such moderation, we are certainly of stone. For myself, I am profoundly affected by it, and therefore have taken occasion to say so in the preface which is inserted before the *Epistle to the Romans*." [2]

Calvin wrote one letter, and one letter only, to Luther, in which he brought before him a matter that gave him considerable anxiety—the necessity there was for the disciples of Christ giving a more decided testimony to their faith. The letter was written, as all Calvin's were, in the most courteous and respectful terms. Luther, however, never received the letter. It had been forwarded to Melanchthon to deliver

[1] Bonnet, Letter 42. [2] *Ibid.*, Letter 42.

to him, but he had not done so. His explanation is not quite satisfactory. "I have not shown your letter to Dr. Martin, for he takes up many things suspiciously, and does not like his replies to questions of the kind you have proposed to him to be carried round and handed from one to another." The last sentence of Calvin's letter to Luther shows how large a *heart* the theologian of Geneva had. "Would that I could fly to you that I might, even for a few hours, enjoy the happiness of your society; for I would prefer, and it would be far better, not only upon this question, but also about others, to converse personally with yourself; but seeing that it is not granted to us on earth, I hope that shortly it will come to pass in the kingdom of God." [1]

II. John Knox took refuge in Geneva when Queen Mary began her reign of terror in England. This was in 1554, when Calvin's power and influence were approaching their zenith. Knox received a hearty welcome in Geneva, and though, as has been usually thought, a few years the senior of Calvin, he venerated the latter as a father. He never felt so happy as when in the company of Calvin.

[1] Bonnet, Letter 124.

He had brought some questions with him on which he desired Calvin's opinion. One was whether a female can preside over and rule a kingdom by divine right, and so transfer the right of sovereignty to her husband. Calvin replied that though female rule was contrary to the legitimate course of nature, it was to be considered among the visitations of the divine anger, although there had been illustrious examples of it like that of Deborah. Yet it should be endured till God put an end to it.[1] This was hardly the answer Knox desired. Calvin, however, would never favour force, robbery, or bloody revolt in such a case: and sorely as his own countrymen afterwards suffered at the hands of the Guises, he repeatedly disowned all sympathy with Amboise and his fellow-conspirators, as his letters to Admiral Coligny and other friends show.[2]

The year following Knox was appointed one of the ministers of the English congregation at Geneva. The Temple *de notre Dame la Neuve* was granted for the joint use of the English and Italian refugees. Knox's colleague was Christopher Goodman. For two years he laboured in Calvin's city, where he found a state of morals and church polity that seemed to him ideal. He

[1] Bonnet, Letter 348. [2] *Ibid.*, Letter 588.

called it a place "whair I nether feir nor eschame to say is the maist perfyt schoole of Chryst that ever was in the erth since the dayis of the Apostillis. In other places I confess Chryst to be trewlie preachit; but maneris and religioun so sinceirlie reformat, I have not yit sene in any uther place."

In 1558 he published in Geneva his *Blast against the Monstrous Regiment of Women.* Although a man of proverbial fearlessness, he published this extraordinary work without the name of author or publisher appearing in their usual place. The issuing of it from Geneva wellnigh brought Calvin into trouble. He had the same year forwarded a copy of his commentary on *Isaiah* to Queen Elizabeth, to whom also he had dedicated the volume. To his surprise the gift was but coldly received, and some harsh words were spoken about him by Cecil, the English Minister. He hastened to put himself right, and wrote to Cecil: "I had no suspicion of the book" (Knox's *Blast*), "and for a whole year was ignorant of its publication. When I was informed of it by certain parties, I sufficiently showed my displeasure that such paradoxes should be published."[1] It is not surprising that Calvin should

[1] Bonnet, Letter 538.

thus throw his friend's work overboard, considering the dictum he had already laid down on the subject, and the wild nature of Knox's attack on female government.

In 1559 Knox wrote from Scotland to Calvin, asking his opinion on other questions. One was whether monks and popish priests, who neither serve the church nor are capable of serving it, although they have renounced their errors, ought to have the annual rents of the church paid to them. Calvin wrote back: "Although those who perform no service in the church had not a just claim to be supported by its funds, still, as the popish clergy had brought themselves under engagements in times of ignorance, and had consumed a part of their lives in idleness, it seemed harsh to deprive them of all support." [1]

The next occasion when sentiments were interchanged between the two men was one that did credit to the kindly heart that beat within Calvin's stormy breast. Marjorie Bowes, Knox's first wife, died in 1561. The marriage had been a happy one; and by it Knox had two sons, both of whom entered the Church of England. Calvin wrote to him a letter in which, in brief but touching words, he expressed his sympathy. "Your

[1] *Calvini Epistolae et Responsa*, Letters 283, 285.

loss," he said, "is a deep and bitter affliction to me. You had a wife to whom few can be compared; but you know well where to find consolation, and I doubt not that you will bear this great sorrow with patience. Greet the pious brethren in my name."[1] In a letter to Goodman of the same month (April 1561) he says: "I grieve not a little that our friend Knox has been deprived of his most sweet wife; but I rejoice that, afflicted as he has been, he has continued to labour strenuously for Christ and the church."[2]

Calvin was superior to Knox in enlightenment and mental breadth. Thus when the latter was vexing his righteous soul over some remnants of popery in the Prayer-book, Calvin advised him not to worry about them, but rather to treat them as "tolerable fooleries." Knox's prayer for the queen, "Enlighten her heart, O Lord, if it be Thy good will," could never have come out of Calvin's mouth. The prim and fastidious Calvin did not approve of personalities of this kind.

Calvin's great and masterful mind exercised a powerful influence over John Knox, and, through him, over Scotland and other lands. In every-

[1] *Calvini Epistolae et Responsa*, Letter 305.
[2] *Ibid.*, Letter 306.

thing that came from Knox's pen, after 1559, in his Liturgy, his Confession of Faith, his book of Discipline, and in his pamphlet on Predestination, we can trace the spirit and the ideas of Geneva. What could be more in Calvin's best manner than these words of Knox's: "But yet I say that the doctrine of God's eternal Predestination is so necessarie to the Church of God, that, without the same, can Faith neither be truely taught, neither surely established, man can never be broght to true humilitie and knowledge of himself; neither yet can he be ravished in admiration of God's eternal goodness, and so moved to praise him as apperteineth. For first, there is no way more proper to buyld and establish faith, than when we heare and undoubtedly do beleve that our Election (which the Spirit of God doth seale in our hartes) consisteth not in ourselves but in the eternal and immutable pleasure of God."[1]

III. If frankness and candour, almost to the verge of unpleasantness, be the sign and seal of true friendship between man and man, the gentle Melanchthon received many proofs of Calvin's friendship for him. In one letter he tells him he is too facile; in another that his

[1] Hume Brown's *Knox*, I. 250.

manner of dissenting from the doctrine of election has greatly shocked him; in another he calls him a timorous man, philosophising too much and theologising too little. Yet was there none whom Calvin loved so dearly, and again and again he makes cordial avowal of his feelings. So notorious was the trust and affection of the two men for each other that the enemy, when he wished to wound their feelings, took a passage from one of their books and gave it a twist so as to make it appear that they contradicted one another. In a letter of indignant protest against a wicked plot of this kind to divide the two friends, Calvin, addressing the Seigneurs of Geneva, says: "He who would place Melanchthon and myself in opposition, greatly wrongs both the one and the other, as well as the whole Church of God. I honour Melanchthon as much on account of the excellent knowledge which is in him, as for his virtues; and more than all, because of his having laboured faithfully to further the gospel. If I find anything to reprove, I do not conceal it from him, as he gives me full liberty not to do so. As for him, there are witnesses more than enough, who know how much he loves me." [1]

[1] Bonnet, Letter 300 (*vid.* Letter 577).

SHORT BIBLIOGRAPHY

I. ORIGINAL AUTHORITIES

Works of Calvin, published by the Calvin Translation Society in 52 volumes. Edinburgh, 1843-55.

Jules Bonnet, *Lettres françaises de Jean Calvin.* 2 vols. Paris, 1854.

English translation of above. Vols. I. II. Edinburgh, 1855. Vols. III. and IV., Philadelphia, 1858.

A. L. Herminjard, *Correspondence des Réformateurs dans le pays de langue française.* Genève, 1866-97.

Joan. Calvini Epistolae et Responsa. Hanoviae, 1597.

II. BIOGRAPHIES

Th. Beza, " Vita Calvini." Translation by Beveridge in *Calvin's Tracts.* Vol. I. Translation Society, Edinburgh, 1844.

Hieron Bolsec, *Histoire de la vie.* Paris, 1577.

Paul Henry, *Das Leben Johann Calvins des grossen Reformators.* Hamburgh, 1835-44. Translation by Stebbing in 2 vols. London, 1854.

F. W. Kampschultz, *Johann Calvin, seine Kirche und sein staat in Genf.* Leipzig, vol. I., 1869; vol. II., 1899.

Thomas McCrie, *The Early Years of John Calvin. A Fragment* (1509-1536). Edinburgh, 1880.

E. Doumergue, *Jean Calvin, Les hommes et les choses de son temps*. Lausanne, 1899-1903.

Williston Walker, *John Calvin*. Heroes of the Reformation series. New York, 1906.

III. LECTURES, SKETCHES, ESSAYS

T. M. Lindsay, *History of the Reformation*. Edinburgh, 1907.

A. M. Fairbairn, *The Cambridge Modern History*, II. Cambridge, 1903.

A. Kuyper, *Calvinism*. The Stone Lectures. Amsterdam and Edinburgh, 1899.

Philip Schaff, *History of the Creeds of Christendom*. London, 1877.

W. Cunningham, *The Reformers and Theology of the Reformation*. Edinburgh, 1862.

J. A. Froude, "Calvinism," *Short Studies*, 2nd series. London, 1877.

G. P. Fisher, *History of Christian Doctrine*. Edinburgh, 1896.

J. A. Wylie, *History of Protestantism*.

John Tulloch, "Calvin" (revised), *Chambers's Encyclopedia*, II. Edinburgh, 1901.

INDEX